D0734679

MONEY^{SHIFT}

MONEYSHIFT

how to **prosper** from what you **can't control**

JERRY WEBMAN

WILEY

John Wiley & Sons, Inc.

Published by John Wiley & Sons, Inc., Hoboken, New Jersey.
Published simultaneously in Canada.

For general information on our other products and services or for technical support, please contact our Customer Care Department within the United States at (800) 762-2974, outside the United States at (317) 572-3993 or fax (317) 572-4002.

Wiley also publishes its books in a variety of electronic formats. Some content that appears in print may not be available in electronic books. For more information about Wiley products, visit our web site at www.wiley.com.

Library of Congress Cataloging-in-Publication Data:

Webman, Jerry A., 1949–
    Moneyshift : how to prosper from what you can't control / Jerry Webman.
        p. cm.
    Includes index.
    ISBN 978-1-118-18140-9 (cloth)
        1. Portfolio management.   2. Investments.   3. Wealth.   I. Title.
    HG4529.5.W433   2012
    332.6—dc23
                                                                    2012004766

Printed in the United States of America

10   9   8   7   6   5   4   3   2   1

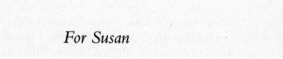

For Susan

Contents

Acknowledgments

For over 30 years I've read with pride and pleasure the acknowledgments authors have addressed to my agent, Susan Ginsburg. The descriptions have a pattern: supportive, tough, fair, funny, creative, loyal, persistent, brilliant, even Superwoman. I repeat them all with emphasis and add my own: beloved. Thanks for kicking me in the pants until I wrote this thing.

I also thank Susan Webman and our four wonderful children, Anna, Rachel, Aaron, and Josh, for contributions to this effort that are as varied as they are.

Many colleagues at OppenheimerFunds have contributed ideas both broad and detailed to the book. I hope I've done them justice. I particularly want to thank Brian Levitt, Lori Heinel, Ashley Felden, James Mehring, Tim Horsburgh, Sarah Beaumont, Sarah Busch, Eliot Walsh, Diane Frankenfield, Ari Gabinet, the Global Equity team (who will recognize the influence of their MANTRA), Alice Fricke, Mike Quinn, Jodi Rabinowitz, Jim O'Connell, and Erin Brunswick, as well as Marty Willis for her support of the project. Bill Glasgall generously contributed both his financial knowledge and his editorial skills to the final manuscript. Leonard Mlodinow rescued me from several errors in physics, demographics, and logic.

Leonard Ginsburg has given me many things more important than help for this book, but in this context I thank him for always helping me see financial issues from a practical, human perspective.

I also thank my John Wiley & Sons editors, Debra Englander, Tula Batanchiev, and Kimberly Bernard, for their contributions to the project. Many others will recognize their thoughts represented and no doubt misrepresented throughout. I thank all of them. Finally, many thanks to Susanna Margolis, whose insights, clarity, and perseverance made her help with the manuscript invaluable. Any errors and omissions are my own.

Introduction

What's Shifting

Did you ever think your ability to pay for your kids' college educations would suffer from a generation of Greeks retiring at an age when most of us are still revving up our careers? Or that the airfare you pay to fly from Chicago to Denver would rise and fall according to the overnight borrowing rate set by the Central Bank of Brazil? Did you ever imagine you'd care about other people getting home mortgages they had no hope of repaying? Or that you'd worry about apartment vacancy rates in Shanghai or the price of onions in New Delhi? Have you wondered why the stock market has a bad case of attention deficit disorder, and why bonds don't pay enough interest to meet the cost of the safe-deposit box you keep them in? Oh, right: that, too, has changed; bond certificates are now wall decorations.

The world is changing, and matters that once seemed remote now shape our lives—and certainly our finances. Many of us are frustrated—even angry—at the result. Depending on which cable news channel you prefer (where have you gone, Walter Cronkite?), you've heard it all: Blame Wall Street! Blame the Fed! Blame Bush! Blame Obama! Blame Europe! Finding someone to blame is not an investment strategy, and this book is about how to come up with an investment strategy that will succeed in bringing you prosperity in the world as it is now, not as you might wish it to be.

I don't recall a time in which we didn't hear that the pace of change was greater than it had ever been, and certainly, change has always been a constant—so constant that it's a cliché. But sometimes we can recognize that something more fundamental than today's headlines has changed, and when that happens, we need to change with it. We acknowledge that necessity in our realization that the tried-and-true methods aren't working so well anymore, in the anger we feel as our expectations are frustrated, and, most importantly, in the success we achieve when we recognize the change and learn to thrive in its wake.

This book is about such a change in the global economy and about the waves that change has churned up in our own lives, especially in the parts of our lives concerned with providing for our financial well-being. Some of us will let those waves of change knock us over; some of us will figure out how to catch a wave or two and ride it back to shore, maybe having a bit of fun on the way. But as this book asserts, if we cannot control those waves, we can still use them to our advantage.

Arriving at the realization that something fundamental has changed and will likely stay that way for some time ranks among the most important and most difficult steps a successful investor can take. I spent almost 30 years of my career as an analyst, portfolio manager, and leader of analysts and portfolio managers. Over those years, the daily flood of financial, economic, and political data went from overwhelming to unfathomable. People like me pay obsessive attention to all this information, misinformation, and disinformation because we both worry and hope that some facts will tell us that an important situation has changed and we need to change our views as a result.

But what if that change is ephemeral, a straw in the wind before things return to normal? The fact that we have so many clichés to describe the (horns of) dilemmas like this one—a rock and a hard place, the frying pan and the fire, Scylla and Charybdis—suggests that we need to proceed cautiously. I've seen experienced investors fail both by clinging to the false hope that some market will "regress to the mean" and by insisting that every surprise meant that "it's different this time." So we'll tread carefully as we decide which elements of what we think we know about investing deserve to be preserved and which merit relegation to the annals of financial history.

Failing to recognize when fundamental change really has occurred doesn't just annoy us and perhaps prompt us to look for scapegoats; it can leave us much poorer than we need to be. My parents began their adult lives during the Great Depression of the 1930s. For my father, that difficult period was only a shadow of the deprivation he had endured during World War I and its aftermath in Eastern Europe. Those combined experiences taught both my parents that good times don't always last and that when it comes to money, safety dominates all other considerations. Through a combination of hard work and thrift (their children would say stinginess), they approached retirement age in the late 1960s with a modest nest egg on which to live out their years.

They'd invested that nest egg safely—in U.S. government savings bonds that paid a couple of percentage points of interest. The problem was that just as my parents' earning years were ending, the Great Inflation was beginning. Their cost of living began to accelerate, and their nest egg began to wither. They sold their home and began living even more frugally. Fortunately, in the mid-1970s, a financial advisor convinced them (convinced me, actually) to move some of their fixed-income positions to dividend-paying stocks, and that action gave them enough inflation cover to remain solvent to the end of their lives. Something had changed, and they had failed, for a time at least, to change with it. Their single-minded pursuit of safety had led them down a path that changing times had made increasingly dangerous.

This book is an attempt to keep you from doing something similar, so that you recognize what has changed and what you can do to prosper from that change. You and I can't control the U.S. housing market, the European sovereign debt crisis, or the repercussions of breakout growth occurring in rapidly growing economies around the world, but that doesn't mean we must be their passive victims, either.

In this book I'll explain why the financial world looks so different from the one we lived in through the last quarter of the twentieth century and the first few years of this one. What was the Great Moderation, and what does it mean that it has ended? I won't be the first to tell you about the stunning growth in countries we once called "emerging markets," but I will tell you how you can seize the enormous investment opportunities they offer without falling into the traps that knee-jerk investment thinking can put in your path. I'll remind you that some of the old-hat, familiar investment opportunities can still work, and I'll show you how to know which ones those are. I'll tell you where your single greatest investment opportunity stands and argue that you need look no farther than the nearest mirror to find it. Finally, I'll help you put these ideas together into a portfolio of investments because getting the right fit between your financial needs and aspirations on the one hand and your portfolio of investments on the other is far more important than sniffing out the few great ideas you can brag to your friends about. I'll add some suggestions about where you can turn for the information and advice you'll need to structure, monitor, and maintain that portfolio.

Why do you need one more investment book? You need it because the world has both changed in important ways and stayed the same in others. Money has shifted geographically, technologically, and demographically, and we need to see how and to explore why it matters. Once we recognize that change has occurred and understand the nature of the change, we can begin to determine how to use the new realities and what remains of the old to gain and protect for ourselves a whole new prosperity.

Chapter 1

Where Has All the Prosperity Gone?

I f you grew up in the America of the latter part of the twentieth century, you probably formed a reasonable expectation that as you grew up and grew older, your wealth would steadily increase and your standard of living would consistently rise.

It was really more than an expectation. Not quite a guarantee, it nevertheless felt something like a promise—part of a social contract between you and the society in which you lived, a covenant you metaphorically entered into at birth as a citizen of the wealthiest country in the world.

Your part of the covenant was to study hard, get as much education as you could stand and afford, find productive employment, and make your contribution to the gross domestic product (GDP), the nation's overall wealth. In return, you would have sufficient wherewithal not just to live comfortably but to save and invest and assure yourself and your family—possibly even your heirs—a continually escalating standard of living. You would invest savings today to have money in the future that you could apply to goals that changed as your life changed: a home of your own, an exciting vacation, a string of college tuition payments, and eventually a secure retirement.

Even though gold watches and comfortable company pensions have been disappearing for years, most commonly you'd look to corporate benefit programs to help with your investing. On-the-job investing typically meant a 401(k) retirement plan, often with matching employer contributions, which allowed you to choose from among a range of investment options, primarily in mutual funds. You might supplement this with your own personal portfolio of investments in equities and fixed-income instruments, and you would probably try to mix up the portfolio in terms of asset class, geography, industry type, and so on as a way of diversifying risk and ensuring reward. Sure, the market value of your account suffered the occasional dip, sometimes a significant one, but over the years, the markets made you more and more prosperous.

And you would likely buy a house. It would probably be your biggest investment, the biggest single asset in your portfolio, the asset you planned to sell when the time came—when the kids were grown and gone and your career was winding down—to fund a secure retirement. Even better, since house prices never seemed to go down, you could spend what you earned—or more—knowing that your house was doing the saving for you.

In fact, owning your own home seemed like something more than just an investment. It, too, felt like part of the covenant. It belonged inherently to the picture we all carried in our heads of the American dream—the career, the house, the expectation of rising prosperity. Compared to your parents, the dream said, your car would be more plush, your house bigger, and your travel more worldly. Maybe your paycheck wouldn't cover this burgeoning lifestyle, but your investment portfolio and your home equity line would cover the gap.

For decades—certainly from the 1980s right through to the end of the twentieth century and just beyond—Americans who held this expectation of rising prosperity were rarely disappointed. The social contract worked; the covenant held. And most of us—again, not unreasonably—began to feel that this was the way things always were and would always be.

And then came the dot-com collapse, the puncturing of the housing bubble, the debacle in the subprime mortgage market, the collapse or near collapse of some of the best-known banks and brokerage houses, and then the Great Recession that followed. And the covenant was smashed to smithereens. Even if you dutifully paid your affordable mortgage, kept your debts under control, and followed the textbook solutions for diversifying your portfolio, your fortunes were caught up in the financial storm. Your monthly financial statements told you so. Not only would your investments not pay for life's luxuries; their disappointing returns threatened to deny you the opportunity eventually to stop working, harvest their growth, and enjoy the lengthy retirement you've spent all those hours on the treadmill—both literally and figuratively—staying in shape for. Suddenly the octogenarian greeting you at the Walmart seemed like the ghost of retirements to come.

Crisis

We all know what happened. We—individuals, families, banks, the government—were leveraged to the hilt with debt that had no real underlying economic value, and when the lenders tested the value of their collateral, there was nothing there. Then as lenders to those lenders began to look more closely at both what they owned themselves and what they suspected their counterparties might own, a very loud financial whistle blew, and the financial system pretty nearly froze in place.

I can give you the date when the crisis began: August 8, 2007. I call it—pardon my French—the "*merde* moment" because that's the day a large French bank realized that it couldn't sell securities it needed to liquidate in order to meet the demand for redemptions from some of its managed accounts. Those accounts held securities tied to U.S. subprime mortgages, and that was the day global markets balked at buying those securities. No market for the securities and hence no redemptions from the accounts meant a liquidity problem for whoever had invested in those accounts. Central banks cranked up the (electronic) printing presses to replace banks' liquidity, but they couldn't hold back the mudslide of asset erosion that followed through the end of the next year from commercial banks, investment banks, and insurance companies that also borrowed and lent.

Moody's Investors Service used to have a plaque over its front door saying, "Credit: Man's Confidence in Man." Once financial institutions lost confidence in each other's balance sheets, credit collapsed, and with the collapse of credit, there went the ability to finance worthy ventures—as well as those not so worthy. Everything tanked. Banks around the world needed bailouts, stock markets plunged, businesses failed, jobs were lost. In the United States, the financial crisis of 2007 ushered in a seven-percentage-point increase in the unemployment rate, leaving us, as I write this some four and a half years later, with more than 14 million people unemployed. The crisis also sparked a 9 percent decline in the output of goods and services produced by labor and property—our gross domestic product—the largest decline since the end of World War II.

Equity prices fell 56 percent over three and a half years, and your 401(k) became, as one wag put it, your 201(k). Visions of a comfortable retirement turned into plans for keeping the old clunker going long enough to sustain a commute for more years to come—if your job didn't disappear in the meantime.

Housing prices declined by 35 percent, a loss in value you're well aware of if you're a homeowner—that is, if you're a homeowner who hasn't sold short, walked away, or been forced into foreclosure.

Let's hold it right there for a moment, because the housing market was the cause, the effect, and for most people the most painful symptom of our disappearing prosperity. Unless your house is very different from the national average, you probably couldn't sell it now for more than it would have fetched nearly a decade ago. If it's like the average American home, it would now sell for about 30 percent less than its peak value in mid-2006. Even if you had no intention of selling your house, even if you had inherited it at birth and had never spent a penny on it, you still felt the impact of the decline in its value. That's because we found a trick to convert our houses into an income-generating investment without putting it up for sale. Why give up the family castle when you could spend part of its ever-increasing value right now, without the risk of having to pack your mother-in-law's silver or your golf clubs into a moving van?

Enter the magic of the home equity loan. We could spend whatever we earned *and more* as long as house prices kept rising and lenders were willing to advance us the increased value in the guise of home equity loans. It was like having an ATM machine on the bathroom wall. Every day the house was worth more than the day before. So every day our home equity credit lines let us get our hands on that value to keep our lifestyle expanding, regardless of our actual take-home pay. Every day—until one fine day when the increased value wasn't there anymore, the ATM machine was empty, and the expanding lifestyle screeched to a halt.

Even though your ATM machine ran dry, the loan that fed it, unless you've already defaulted or paid it off, is still in some financial institution's vault—along with all the other primary and secondary mortgages that were secured by real estate prices that are now a distant memory. Those remaining piles of impaired mortgages leave bankers less willing to lend to one another and less able to lend to the public. The homeowners who still keep those mortgages current can't readily move or refinance or buy many of the goods and services your company or the company you've invested in wants to sell them.

In other words, since the financial crisis of 2007, wealth has been draining from the economy and away from you, and financially speaking, you're stagnant. Even if you've lived within your means, even if you're still able to afford your house or have paid off your mortgage, and even if your stock portfolio is holding its own—no mean feat in a market as volatile and disappointing as this one—it's unlikely that your wealth is growing through these investments. Even the prudent and thrifty among us are disappointed because when everyone else in America lacked the means to consume more and more each year, an engine driving the whole economy sputtered—and investments geared to our domestic growth sputtered with it.

It's equally unlikely that your income is keeping pace with the rising cost of living—exemplified most dramatically by the continually climbing prices for energy and food, two essentials. In fact, between 2000 and 2010, the average American's per capita income, after taxes and adjusted for overall inflation, increased just over $4,000;[1] that's the kind of money that is easily eaten up by higher prices at the grocery store and the pump—not to mention at the doctor's office—all places where prices have gone up more than the headline averages. Having worked for 10 years and found that we have only another $4,000 in purchasing power means that our ability to provide for even modestly expanded needs and aspirations is barely within our reach.

Life feels very much like being on a treadmill: You work and work, you keep on contributing to your retirement plan and feeding your portfolio, you pay your mortgage and your other bills, and still your personal treasury gets no bigger.

Solutions? The ones we used to rely on don't seem to provide the results they once did. The standard diversification fix for volatility in financial markets doesn't work when all the financial markets seem to rally or collapse together. However many baskets we put our eggs in, they all seemed to have a hole in the bottom.

You could look for a scapegoat. People doing just that are beating drums a few blocks from my New York financial district office. It's easy to blame Wall Street, banks, and bankers, and the public as a whole has angrily and vociferously done just that, growing especially enraged when we learned that after receiving taxpayer bailouts, individual bankers were continuing to give themselves huge compensation packages. "Compensation for what?" a furious public wanted to know—"Risking our depositor money recklessly with the assurance you wouldn't be the ones to suffer the consequences?" Even the Academy Awards offered an opportunity for a recipient who had written and directed an exposé of Wall Street's sins to call for the jailing of the financial executives responsible.

Political leaders in droves climbed on the bank-bashing bandwagon. Or they spent so much time amping up attacks on each other that they nearly let the country default on its own debt. Or they asserted that the financial stagnation and the smashing of the covenant you relied on were the fault of the government. Taxes are too high, or they're too low, or they're levied on the wrong people. Or blame China. Or globalization. Perhaps. Political debates and government processes are rarely encouraging things to watch—recall Bismarck's famous line that if you want to keep your respect for laws and sausages, avert your eyes from seeing how both are made. But our debate has degenerated into a pitiful spectacle of name-calling and sloganeering. Listening to your favorite finger-wagging pundit on TV may make you feel better, but it won't grow your assets.

Or you could just wait it out. History tells us that it takes about a decade for output, unemployment, and housing values to recover after a financial crisis. That was certainly the case with the housing boom that went bust in the 1980s. Prices dropped consistently for about three years after the bubble burst, but a decade later, houses had recovered all their value, and by about 1998, prices were well beyond their old levels. True, the bubble that followed, the bubble that simply ballooned in the early years of the twenty-first century, was bigger and faster than that 1980s bubble—and its puncturing was correspondingly more explosive. But the weight of history suggests that housing values do reach a point where they really have no place to go but up. Presumably, if you can hang on until 2020 or so, all your investment assets will again be on a path of growth.

Or, if you'd rather not wait, there is another way. Invest for the reality of what is—not for what was or what you think ought to be. There is a whole new level of prosperity to be found in what you can't control.

Reality Bites

The reason the old solutions for investment success aren't working today is that they were based on an investing perspective that was inherently specious. The first thing to do, therefore, is to disenthrall yourself from that old perspective. Toss out the covenant. The idea of continually rising prosperity falling into your lap—virtually without your lifting a finger—is gone. In fact, it was a figment of our collective imagination in the first place, and, as it turns out, it was inspired by a fluke. That period of time in which most of us matured financially—specifically, the quarter century between 1982 and 2007—was so special, in an aberrant way, that economists have given it a name. They call it the Great Moderation. Far from being the way things always were and always would be, the Great Moderation was a one-off, an anomaly. To plan for our future, we need to begin by understanding what this anomaly was about and why it had to end.

Market volatility, when it occurred during this period, was modest, and it was brief. It fired up, then faded. The result was what I call the Goldilocks Environment—never too hot, never too cold, always just right for investing. That had not happened before, and it has not happened since.

But it wasn't just lack of volatility that distinguished the Great Moderation; it also represented a stunning respite from the kind of uncertainty that typically prevails in the financial world. While recent television has revived nostalgia for the immediate post–World War II period, the era was actually riddled with financial uncertainty. The man in the gray flannel suit who symbolized the 25-year period between 1948 and 1973 faced a recession every four and a quarter years on average. With unemployment rising to 6 percent five times during the period,[2] he worried frequently about losing his job. When he did enjoy a period of economic growth, it lasted on average only about four years.[3]

Yet these vagaries of the business cycle seemed tolerable compared to the extended period that followed, when inflation gripped the U.S. economy and stifled its growth. This was an ugly period that whelped an ugly term—stagflation.

Remember the 1970s? Those who do will recall that the price of a loaf of bread cost a nickel more every time you made a trip to the supermarket. Every can of soup had two or three price stickers on top of each other marking successive price increases. Wages continued to ratchet up as well, often driven by cost-of-living pay contracts, but higher wages didn't buy more goods and services. Instead, with wages tied to prices, both rose together, so as the paycheck got bigger, so did the bills for groceries, rent, and clothing. The result was that consumers were no better off while businesses struggled to earn a profit. Our standard of living melted away like your polyester leisure suit when hit by the ashes of whatever you were smoking.

And because businesses failed to grow, the stock market languished. The Dow Jones Industrial Average first broke the 1,000 barrier in late 1972 and reached 1,050 the following January. The index fell below 580 late in 1974 and didn't reach 1,050 again until early 1983: Cash in and cash out, you were back where you had started from 10 years earlier. But a decade of inflation meant that investing $1,050 in 1973 and spending $1,050 in 1983 were two very different things, because by 1983, you needed about $2,355 to buy what $1,050 would have bought in 1973. You would have been better off spending than investing in the Dow. See? Disco music wasn't the only bad thing about the 1970s.

The end of the inflationary plague is legend and reflects the political courage of two Presidents, Jimmy Carter, who in 1979 first appointed Paul Volcker as Federal Reserve chairman, and Ronald Reagan, who reappointed Volcker in 1983. Volcker apparently read the book on monetary policy and recognized that measures like wage and price controls and WIN buttons—for "Whip Inflation Now"—wouldn't stop the price spiral; only a monetary starvation diet for the economy would do the trick. The way central banks like the Federal Reserve cause us to starve for money is to make it really expensive for both individuals and businesses to borrow it.

Under Volcker's leadership, the Federal Reserve pushed the rate at which commercial banks lent money to each other overnight (the Fed funds rate) from 11 percent to 20 percent. Banks depend on this very short-term funding for the cash they need to lend money to you, me, and the businesses they deal with. With banks' funding costs this high, the interest rates they charged borrowers also reached daunting levels. Money is like oranges: The more it costs, the less we want of it; and the less money there is circulating through the economy, the less likely it is that the things that require money will happen. Borrowing and lending, buying and selling, expanding and hiring all cratered. With jobs scarce and sales shrinking, businesses couldn't raise prices, and employees couldn't demand wage increases. Inflation began to wither. Two severe recessions later, price stability had returned.

To all of this—the nearly 40 years of volatility, stagflation, and uncertainty—the arrival of the Great Moderation seemed like salve to a wound. Figure 1.1 illustrates how the contrast between that period and the volatile periods of short business cycles, inflation worries, and shaky markets that came before could hardly have been greater, and it shows us what has come since. For the 25 years between 1982 and 2007, inflation ranged between a high of 6 percent and a low of 3 percent. The best stretch came between 1992 and 2005 when inflation never topped 4 percent—and rarely fell below 1.5 percent.

U.S. CPI and Real GDP Growth, Year-over-Year Change

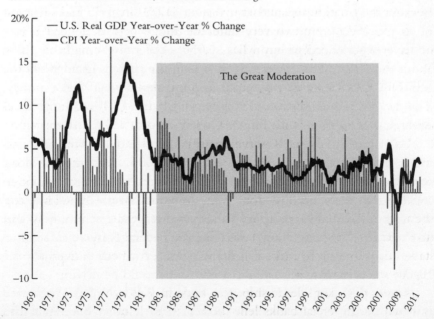

Figure 1.1   The Great Moderation: Economic Growth and Inflation
SOURCE OF CHART DATA: Bloomberg, 2011.

Keeping inflation within that tight and steady range benefited individuals and businesses alike. When you went to buy groceries, clothing, or even a car during those years, you pretty much knew what each item would cost, and if you put off a purchase, you could figure the price wouldn't change that much. And if you operated a business, your wage and inventory costs were stable enough that you could plan for expansions and hire workers without the fear that your costs would soar or that your selling price would collapse.

Yes, we had two brief recessions, one in 1990–1991 following the real estate bubble, oil price spikes, and the first Gulf War, and a second in 2001 following the dot-com bubble. But even during those fairly brief periods when the U.S. economy shrank, the GDP never slipped more than 0.2 percent on an annual basis, which constitutes a pretty small contraction compared to what came before and after. There were only four calendar quarters from the beginning of 1983 to the end of 2007 during which the total value of all the goods and services in the U.S. economy actually declined; in contrast, we saw five between 2007 and the start of 2012.

If those few months when business slowed and jobs were lost could be called adversity, I think most of us would welcome it today. Why? Because the times before and after that so-called adversity brought most of us more economic security than we had ever experienced before or have experienced since. In fact, perhaps the most remarkable thing about the Great Moderation was how long the periods lasted when the economy grew, jobs were plentiful, and businesses could make money. The longest period on record during which the U.S. economy grew without interruption began in March 1991 and lasted for 10 years.[4]

As Figure 1.2 shows, the stock market (represented by the S&P 500 index) was also on a pretty steady run until 2000, tracking right along with home prices. The good times rolled. I splurged on a $12,000 car in 1982. Suppose I'd been content with the average early 1980s ride and spent about half that much[5] and then invested the rest in a way that just kept pace with the Dow Jones Industrial Average. By 2007, I would have been able to sell my stocks and plunk down the money for the BMW roadster that my son-in-law thinks I should be driving.

From 1981 until the tech bubble burst in 2000, the Dow registered just two negative years. Even the crash of 1987 left us with a small gain for the year. In fact, the Dow's average return between 1983 and 2007 was almost 10.7 percent; had you reinvested all your dividends during

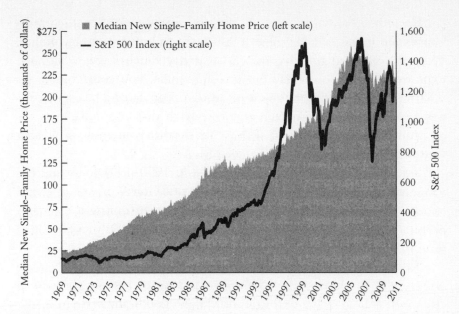

Figure 1.2   The Great Moderation: Equity and Housing Markets
SOURCE OF CHART DATA: Haver Analytics, 2011.

that period, you would have realized an annual return of a bit more than 13.75 percent— a really good return. The Dow index was at 1,046 at the end of 1982 and had climbed to 13,265 by the end of 2007. And of course the old homestead just kept getting more and more valuable. Ah, for the good old days.

What about inflation? It's true that in 2007, you needed about $2,250 to buy the same goods and services you could have bought for $1,050 in 1982. But if you had invested that $1,050 in 1982 and had earned the return on the Dow, by 2007 you'd have had the purchasing power of about $6,173 in 1982 dollars, both canceling out the inflationary loss and leaving you money to buy a trunkload more of goodies than you could have purchased 25 years earlier. So while I drove my 1982 Olds into the ground, more foresighted folks who had stayed in the market were buying Beemers and Armani suits to wear while driving them. And remember: You made that money just by holding on and ignoring events like the crash of 1987 and the tech wreck of 2000. All you had to do was show up; the stock market rose on its own.

The investment returns of the Great Moderation, especially the continuing boom in the price of our homes, allowed many thrifty, thoughtful people to enjoy a standard of living that their own labor alone could not have provided—by any definition a very good thing. Those investment gains paid for some folks' fancy cars and designer clothes. They also allowed those of us who had lived paycheck-to-paycheck to borrow against our rising home value and take a vacation, fix up the house, or send our kids to private college. The downside was that the magnitude of the returns and the length of time during which we enjoyed them managed to convince us that such investment returns were normal, to be expected, or even owed to us.

How wrong we were, and no wonder we're angry. Since the economy bottomed out in the spring of 2009, we've had a weak but continuing economic recovery. Overall price inflation hasn't been a problem; in fact, deflation seriously threatened the economy for the first time in over 70 years.

Now look at what's happening in the stock market. In October 2007, the Dow hit its all-time high of 14,164 before closing out the year at 13,264. A little over a year later, in March 2009, it hit a low of 6,547. Since that low, we've had a weak but continuing economic recovery with low overall price inflation, yet despite a solid recovery from that low, you still would have been better off spending your money back in October 2007 than investing it in a way that tracked the returns of the Dow ever since. And you didn't hear it here first. Housing prices are on average down some 30 percent from their peaks. Depending on location, prices may still be declining.

For anyone investing in the market, there's a simple bottom line to all this: The Great Moderation is over. Look back on it with nostalgia as a pleasant peculiarity you were just lucky enough to grab a piece of. Then close your eyes and kiss it good-bye.

Spell It D-E-B-T

But surely economies rebound. Stock markets recover. The question is when. Two years after the crash of 1987, the Dow was back to its precrash level. Not bad. After it plunged from the high it hit early in 2000, however, it took six and a half years to regain all it had lost. Not so good. Still, one plan of action for investors might well be to just wait, expecting—as I do—that eventually it will again be possible to profit from holding investments akin to the familiar U.S. stock market indexes. That "eventually," however, could be a long time coming.

Another plan of action, therefore—the one I'll articulate and advocate in this book—recognizes that times have changed and that investment strategies must change as well. No one can promise you how financial markets will behave, and you should ignore anyone who tries, but if we can understand what went right and then went wrong, we can begin to see how the world economy is shifting. Once we get that right, we can begin figuring out how to profit from those shifts.

What has changed? What was so aberrant about the Great Moderation that today we can understand it as an anomaly and be pretty sure that it will not come back—at least not where and how it once resided? What went on in that quarter century that made it so very easy for so very many people to become financially successful in a way that was simply not possible before or since?

The answer is that there was a financial vaccine that kept the Great Moderation going, and now, like an antibiotic up against a resistant strain of bacteria, that vaccine has lost its potency. The vaccine's name? Debt. The doctor administering the vaccine? The Federal Reserve. You can see the pattern in Figure 1.3. Here's the story.

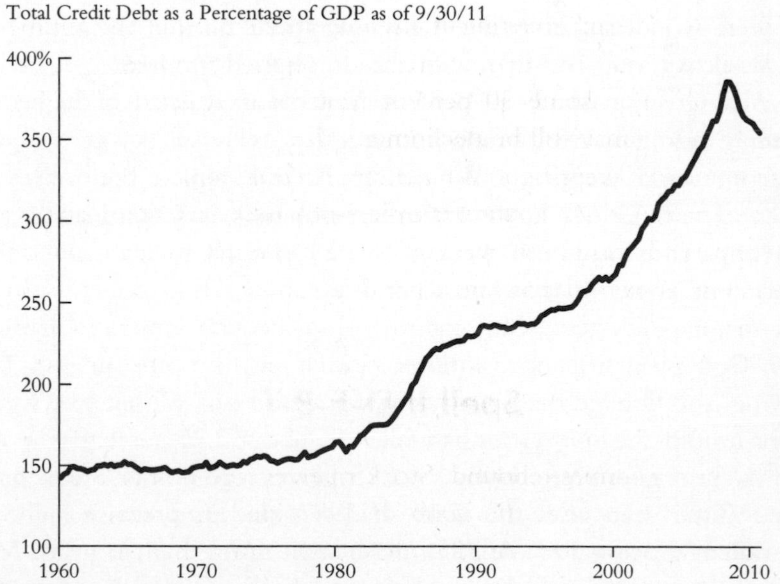
Total Credit Debt as a Percentage of GDP as of 9/30/11
400%
350
300
250
200
150
100
1960
1970
1980
1990
2000
2010

Figure 1.3 The Great Moderation: Debt

SOURCE OF CHART DATA: Ned Davis Research, Inc., September 30, 2011. Copyright 2012 Ned Davis Research, Inc. Further distribution prohibited without prior permission. All Rights Reserved. See NDR Disclaimer at www.ndr.com/copyright.html. For data vendor disclaimers refer to www.ndr.com/vendorinfo.

Several historically unique developments came together at one time to bring the Great Moderation into existence and to keep it going for as long as it endured: the baby boom generation maturing from trouble-making youth to productive adulthood, the flow of immigrants with needed capabilities ranging from no-skill laboring power to very high intellectual and technical skills, the advance and proliferation of information and communication technology, and the end of the Cold War. The convergence of these unique developments, like the proverbial perfect storm, produced truly stunning prosperity. Along the way, however, financial crises threatened to bring back the boom-bust cycles of the earlier postwar period or the grinding inflation of the 1970s. At such moments, our Federal Reserve stepped in, tweaking policy time and again to moderate the impact of these crises.

A prime example took place in October 1987. On October 19 of that year, the Dow Jones Industrial Average fell more than 22 percent—a decline only one percentage point less than the combined drop of October 28 and 29 in 1929, the legendary Great Crash leading to the Great Depression. By the end of that October day in 1987, the pundits were forecasting the next Great Depression, and Wall Streeters like me were wondering if we'd all be selling apples on the sidewalk before the week was out. But then a champion stepped forward.

Alan Greenspan had replaced Paul Volcker as chairman of the Federal Reserve in August 1987, an appointment that, as I recall, was greeted with a fair amount of skepticism. Who, after all, could replace the hero of the inflation wars? Critics, however, underestimated Mr. Greenspan because he'd apparently read both chapters of the monetary policy handbook—what to do about inflation and what to do about a financial crisis. In the first major policy test of his chairmanship, Federal Reserve Chairman Alan Greenspan suspended interest rate targets, thus encouraging borrowing, and flooded the financial system with cash. Within two weeks, three-month Treasury yields had fallen by about 2.25 percentage points and 30-year rates were down by 1.15 percentage points. Stock prices rose. Within two years, the Dow had regained its precrash high; the equivalent process after the 1929 crash took more than 25 years. Most importantly, after the Fed's tweaking, the U.S. economy continued to grow for another three years until the oil price shock and Gulf War finally tipped us into recession.

I'm going to tell two jokes in this book. You'll have to read to the end to find the other one, but this one promises to be a real knee-slapper because it combines the humorous qualities of the University of Chicago (which undergraduates call "the place where fun went to die") with those of the economics profession, and of course economics is known as "the dismal science." Here is the joke produced by those two comic traditions:

Professor Milton Friedman, the Nobel Prize–winning theorist of monetary economics, is lecturing. He notices a student sleeping in the back row and of course calls on him. The student jerks awake and says, "I didn't hear the question, Mr. Friedman, but the answer is 'control the growth rate of money.'"

Done laughing? Here's what's not funny: Throughout the Great Moderation, the Federal Reserve essentially had the same answer: Control the growth rate (or price) of money, and all will be well.

That was the pattern set from the start of Greenspan's Fed chairmanship. Whatever the real or perceived crisis we faced—recessions and weak recoveries early in the 1990s and the 2000s, the Russian government debt default and a huge hedge fund collapse in the late 1990s, the specter of Y2K, or the reality of 9/11—the Greenspan Fed had a monetary response: It would either lower interest rates or print money, or do both.

Every time it did, a particular market roared. In the late 1980s, it was real estate and junk bonds—high-yield debt to its friends. It was the dot-coms a decade later. And a decade after that, it was housing. You didn't have to hear the question to know the answer, and the Fed got straight A's.

Let's come back to the vaccine that made Fed policy so effective: debt. Behind each of these asset booms was an unprecedented rise in private-sector debt—the money that businesses borrow and the money we borrow on our credit cards, our home equity lines, and our car loans. Sure, with the economy growing and the United States producing more and more, you would expect borrowing to increase along with that growth. If I'm earning more money and adding about the same amount to my debt burden, I still might be okay. But as a country, our indebtedness was growing faster than the speed at which we made more and did more. Just take a look in Figure 1.3, which compares the amount of debt we took on to how much the economy was growing—that is, private debt as a percentage of GDP. During the years following World War II, this important ratio rose steadily in the United States—especially in the years after about 1982, the years of the Great Moderation. When growth lagged, the Fed eased the money supply, which in turn made easy credit, which in turn made for market exuberance.

The system worked in reverse as well. If the economy threatened to overheat, to grow too fast and rekindle inflation, the Fed would force up interest rates, making it more difficult and more expensive to borrow. Once things settled down a bit, rates could fall again, and growth would resume its dependable, moderate pace.

Greenspan's ability to use the Federal Reserve's monetary policy powers to conduct the economy's crescendos and diminuendos like an orchestra earned him the sobriquet "Maestro." Speed the economy up or slow it down: The entire strategy depended on credit—on making us more or less willing to borrow and the banks more or less willing to lend. As long as supplying and withholding credit was what drove or slowed the economy, Maestro Greenspan and his successor conductor, Ben Bernanke, could continue to fiddle with monetary policy and control the economy.

But what do monetary policy and the Great Moderation of the economy have to do with our investments? The answer comes back to the basics of risk and return. Suppose I offer you an investment with an expected return of 10 percent a year but, I warn you, with a tendency for its value to bounce around a fair amount. You might be willing to take a risk on it, but you'll probably want to risk a lot less money than if I give you reason to believe that the investment's value will rise that same amount in the future, but smoothly and consistently, without lurching or swaying this way and that. Investors—and therefore markets—like predictability and fear volatility.

Translate that love of predictability to the way stock markets and real estate markets ran up during the past decade, and you'll see why times felt so good. Anytime anyone figures out how to make the future more predictable, investors are happy to put more money at risk. More money means more demand. More demand means higher prices. Higher prices make investors richer, and getting richer encourages them to put more money at risk. And so it goes on and on—as long as somehow we can keep the market from gyrating too wildly.

That's exactly what the Federal Reserve had done, repeatedly and with stunning success, during the Great Moderation: It reduced volatility, seemed to reduce the risk of losing money, and thus reduced investors' fear. Remember the people flipping unbuilt condos in Florida? Their fear was gone—and their judgment with it. So great was the Fed's success in doing this that the pundits began to talk about something they called the "Greenspan put." A put is a financial contract that gives the holder of a security the right to sell it to someone else at a prearranged price, usually below the prevailing market price. The owner of the put has to pay that someone else for the option to sell and protect against eventual losses in the market, but having that protection makes the owner more willing to buy the security covered by the put in the first place. Again: less perceived risk, more demand, higher prices, happy investors. Would you be more likely to buy a pair of chic shoes if you knew that someone was contractually obligated to pay you a preset price for your fashion statement even if they pinched too much to be wearable? Yes, of course you would.

In the financial markets you'll pay a price to buy a put, somewhat like an insurance premium, but the Greenspan put the pundits talked about was a gift from the central bank, a sort of gold-plated toaster. It was, in effect, an assurance to investors. The assurance was that the Fed would act as needed to keep markets from gyrating too violently and keep us from losing money. So in a very real sense, we all enjoyed the benefit of the Greenspan put just by waking up each morning.

When the subprime mortgage situation and credit crunch became a crisis in the late summer of 2007 and banks around the world were gyrating so violently they were on the verge of collapse, the Fed and other major central banks knew what to do; they'd heard the joke: Lower interest rates and print money. Invoke the Greenspan put to settle the markets down. And so they did exactly that—lowered interest rates and printed money.

The problem was that it didn't work this time. At first the stock markets' collective knee jerked upward, but within weeks, far from settling down, the markets continued to gyrate—downward. A year after the first Fed easing of the money supply, the Dow was in fact more than 17 percent lower and had much further to fall. Major financial institutions began to fail, some money market funds threatened to return less than $1.00 per share to their investors, and the financial world seemed on the brink of collapse.[6] Financial institutions were unable or unwilling to extend credit; they were too concerned with maintaining sufficient liquidity to keep themselves afloat without taking on the risk of lending to even the more creditworthy of borrowers.

To their credit, the Federal Reserve and other governmental agencies around the world (and across U.S. administrations) recognized that extraordinary steps were needed to avoid complete financial collapse and to prop up staggering economies and financial markets. In a very real sense, their actions worked: Many financial markets have stabilized and even rallied. But the ongoing sovereign debt issue in Europe underscores the reach and persistence of the damage done in 2007 and 2008, and it highlights the extent to which uncertainty still reigns. So although the financial markets are partially back, the Great Moderation is not and won't be. The bottom line is that no one can promise you dependable investment returns from the old, familiar strategies you counted on for so long. That's the change in the financial reality, and it's why, if you want to prosper from investing, it's time to move forward.

Now What Will We Do?

Open your eyes to a new world of investment possibilities. For if you invest in the way the world works—not the way you wish it would work—the winnings can be lush. The opportunity for wealth hasn't gone away; it has simply moved. A seismic shift in the world's economic momentum has transformed the picture of global growth as surely and as dramatically as any collision of tectonic plates transforms the earth's geology. You can't change it; you *can* make money from it.

Figure 1.4 shows the new picture of global growth with recent annualized rates of growth around the world. The contrasts are stark.

The centers of growth and therefore the opportunities for investment are in the emerging economies, the very places that own the headlines today—for good reason. While we in North America, Western Europe, and Japan stumble over inherent impediments to growth that cannot be cured by our usual policy panaceas, the emerging economies possess the natural, institutional, and demographic resources to extend their growth advantage for decades.

One fact alone illustrates the opportunity: Every year, an estimated 120 million to 130 million people in the developing world leave subsistence agriculture behind and become consumers. Put another way, every two and a half years, a number of people equal to the population of the United States starts to produce enough to buy basic consumer goods and services—clothes, shoes, kitchen utensils, MP3 players, laundry detergent, toys for their kids, furniture, haircuts. That's a lot of people and a lot of goods and services. It is an enormous appetite aborning, with

GDP Growth Year-over-Year as of 9/30/11

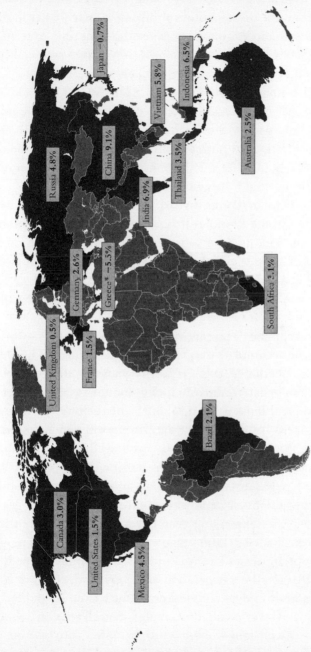

Japan −0.7%

Indonesia 6.5%

Vietnam 5.8%

Russia 4.8%

China 9.1%

Australia 2.5%

Thailand 3.5%

India 6.9%

Germany 2.6%

Greece* −5.5%

South Africa 3.1%

United Kingdom 0.5%

France 1.5%

Brazil 2.1%

Canada 3.0%

United States 1.5%

Mexico 4.5%

Figure 1.4 The New World of Global Growth

GDP (gross domestic product) is the total value of all final goods and services produced in a country in a given year.

*Greece GDP as of March 31, 2011.

SOURCE OF CHART DATA: Bloomberg, September 30, 2011.

enormous value to be created in feeding that appetite and with a vast demand for the capital to create that value. That is the investment opportunity, and because the appetite is aborning so much faster in these economies than it ever did in ours, now is just the right time to seize the opportunity.

The developed countries still control much of the intellectual and financial capital the emerging world needs. Your own skills and capabilities are part of that intellectual capital. Your savings and investment portfolio are certainly part of the financial capital. This book is about how you can make both grow substantially by investing where the new global potential now is. In other words, right now you're in a position to prosper from what you can't change. This book tells you how.

To start with, here are some caveats, because obviously, to make money by investing in the world as it is, you will need to risk money, and that means you need to take some care. Caveat one: The money you invest should be money you don't need for a while. Caveat two: It should be money you can afford to lose—at least some of it anyway, and at least for some time. Caveat three: You need to be prepared to assume a certain level of risk.

If you can accept these caveats, you're ready. If you can't, read Chapter 8 so you can accumulate the capital you need to get ready. Here's some straight talk, whether you listen to my views or someone else's: Investing, unless you're extraordinarily lucky, cannot absolve you of the need to earn, save, and build a financial safety net before you take significant investment risk. In Chapter 9 I suggest ways in which you might realize some value from that cushion, but you'll need it just the same.

Some years ago, a friend came into a financial windfall (no one died; he sold a book to a publisher). He was always in financial straits, and he asked me how he could invest his advance on royalties to finally get out of money trouble. After explaining that I was legally prohibited from giving him investment advice, I did suggest one surefire method to grow his wealth by about 18 percent a year—a bit less than he'd hoped, but okay. What was that surefire advice? "Pay off every penny of your credit card debt," I told him. End of conversation, but I hope he did it.

Once armed, however, with the savings that allow you to begin increasing your risk and lengthening your horizon, you will be in a position to look for entities that need capital—that is, your investment— to create economic value that will exceed that of your investment. These are likely to be entities with access to a strong or expanding market and that produce or provide something that can command a premium in that market. Think of selling a better motorbike to a population that's hurrying to a new job, or cell phones in a place where communications are limited. These businesses should be solid enough not to steal or have stolen from them the value they create. Think of a prestigious brand or a software code that can't easily be broken. And they should be sufficiently in need of capital to offer you an upside good enough to offset the risk you're taking. Once the wall of money has hit the best of investment ideas and pushed its price to fantasy levels, it's time to look elsewhere for another opportunity.

I'll show you where and how to look for these investment opportunities—what to watch for and what to watch out for, how to change your thinking as you put together not just an investment strategy but a comprehensive plan for your financial future.

It won't be as easy as investing used to be during the Great Moderation in which many of us came of age financially. But it offers the opportunity not just to stay ahead of a stagnant economy but to share in the wealth of ascending economies and of growing segments of more developed and familiar markets as well. After all, some of us baby boomers have saved a few bucks or yen or euros and are ready to spend it on our health and leisure. You can make these gains your gain as well, riding our demand for everything from cruises to hearing aids to a higher standard of living for yourself and your family.

The first essential matter is to look at the way the world really works and confront the realities you can't change.

The Bottom Line

Between 1982 and 2007, the United States benefited from an unusually stable economic and financial environment. We call that unusual period the Great Moderation. It was an anomaly, and it's over.

Among the causes of the Great Moderation, the Federal Reserve's success in conducting monetary policy stands out; remember the Maestro. The Fed's ability to regulate the economy depended on its ability to regulate the rate at which private borrowing increased. The Great Moderation ended in the fall of 2007 when the global financial system could no longer absorb additional U.S. debt. Recession became a prolonged reality; deflation threatened; financial markets gyrated.

The likely impact on you: Your prosperity is probably not growing, despite your having put your money in the surest and safest of investments. Pointing the finger at a scapegoat—or at several scapegoats—will not help you achieve financial prosperity. Blame is not an investment strategy.

What now? We all must adjust our thinking and invest where the financial growth is, not where it used to be. To prosper, we'll all need to understand the potential of geographical places, kinds of markets, and product and service enterprises many of us may find unfamiliar.

This book will help make those opportunities understandable.

Chapter 2

What You Can't Control

F irst the party, then the hangover.

That's as certain in investing as in life. Maybe you were one of those investors who woke up after the 2007–2009 financial crisis with a throbbing headache, a sour stomach, and the fervent resolution that you would never let this happen to you again. You knew you had overindulged; you probably knew it as you were doing it, but the way the value of everything you touched just kept rising made it seem crazy not to take just one more sip. And now you were paying the piper.

So you did what history suggests is the thing to do after such excess: You fled to safety. First, you probably started to save more of what you earned. That was smart. In 2005, the average American spent about 99 percent of income earned. Since the crisis, we've been saving between 3 and 5 percent—not quite the average Chinese level, which approaches 30 percent, but an improvement nonetheless. Our debts have shrunk relative to our income—partly because we paid off some

23

debt and partly because our creditors wrote some off. All told, our financial situation is, on average, a bit less precarious than it was a few years ago. So far, so good—but what next? Most of us still need our wealth to grow faster than our savings, and many of us aren't yet on an investment path that will meet that need.

If, like many people, your overwhelming concern became avoiding any possible loss, much of what you've saved is hiding under the mattress or in bank accounts, money market funds, and other seemingly safe havens. These were and are the obvious, predictable reactions to the crisis and hangover of 2007–2009 and to the volatile markets in the years that followed, and if that's what you did, you joined a long line of investors down the centuries. Money under the mattress is, ironically, an effective way to get a good night's sleep.

The problem is: It isn't really working. If you stashed your investable resources in savings accounts, you at least didn't stay awake nights worrying about loss of principal, but your investment grew so slowly that it never caught up with inflation, even low levels of inflation. The dollars you earned didn't buy as much today as they did yesterday, and they'll buy even less tomorrow. Let's not talk about what that hidden treasure will buy in a decade or two. Just suppose that debt-ridden governments, such as the United States, decide to employ the time-honored mechanism of inflation to pay off old debts with new, devalued money. Not an imminent threat in my opinion, this is nonetheless a danger that makes your money-stuffed mattress uncomfortably lumpy. In other words, safety brings its own considerable risks; there is no one single safe-for-all-possibilities investment.

The crisis was predictable, the hangover was predictable, and your response was predictable. But the predictably expected results were not forthcoming. Why? Because it turns out that there is a difference between what is predictable and what is recognizable, and this time around, predictable actions were producing unrecognizable outcomes.

That is why the first step to the rising standard of living this book promises you is to see the world in a fresh way. In Chapter 1, I said we must "disenthrall ourselves," a phrase I stole from Abraham Lincoln. One hundred and thirty-five years after Lincoln, Steve Jobs said something similar: "Think different," Jobs exhorted, with better inspiration than grammar. Either way, both men meant for us to get rid of encrusted assumptions and liberate our brains from old perceptions. It's the crucial baseline step for everything else this book is about. The world has certainly seen financial crises and hangovers before—many times. This one isn't different in theory, just in its particular facts. That's where we have to start.

Predictable versus Recognizable

Research on the history of financial crises confirms that the cycle of crisis and hangover is almost a generational event. The symptoms we have been experiencing since 2007–2009—reduced output, high unemployment, declining asset prices—are all pretty much in line with what researchers tell us has occurred for centuries in every developing or developed economy on every continent on earth—except Antarctica, which has no economy of its own.

From the debasement of the Byzantine gold coin in the eleventh century to the subprime mortgage disaster and credit crunch triggering our own Great Recession in the twenty-first, economies have foundered, fallen, and eventually gotten back on their feet with surprising regularity. Equally surprising is the consistency—almost the uniformity—of the duration of these disasters: The hangover typically lasts for some 5 to 10 years.

Deleveraging—unwinding all that private debt—is a slow process, and the effects are somewhat unexpectedly uniform across the times and places where the deleveraging occurs. In their monumental study of financial crises, Carmen Reinhart and Kenneth Rogoff find that when debt-driven asset bubbles finally burst, a set of financial and economic phenomena follow. Housing and equity prices fall on average 35 and 55 percent, respectively. National economic output falls an average of 9 percent, while unemployment rises 7 percentage points. Overall economic activity improves before employment does—not surprisingly, given that hiring a human being is one of the riskiest things a business can do—but both economic and employment recoveries take several years. And, measured over the past 65 years, government debt rises an average of 65 percent. That's 65 percent without counting increases in future guarantees—we call them entitlements—that governments offer to cushion the blow of all these deprivations.[1]

Does all that sound familiar? The depth and duration of the downturns bring to mind the biblical seven lean years that Joseph divined from the Pharaoh's dream. Repairing our balance sheets, figuring out what a piece of real estate is worth, getting the confidence to expand a business—all these things take time and can't be wished or legislated away. I'm not, by the way, trying to excuse governments' actions that may have prolonged or exacerbated these economic problems, although history does make the U.S. and peripheral European debt problems understandable, if no less challenging.

Nor am I suggesting that we passively wait for things to get back to a familiar pattern that isn't going to return. Neither the fact that the hangover is predictable nor the certainty that it will end someday in no way means that what replaces the hangover will look like anything we have encountered before. Yes, there are new paths that lead to real opportunity, but they are in places we don't know well. Moreover, dramatic shifts in the global political and social equilibrium—shifts we have not seen in our lifetimes—are now driving the opportunity before us. These unrecognizable shifts in unfamiliar places are the reason some economies, like Brazil's, are growing and some, like Italy's, are not. They are the reason investors need to understand as much as they can of what's behind the changes and the directions in which they are taking the world. Two in particular carry profound importance where investing is concerned: the rise of the emerging market (EM) and the aging of the population.

Again, on their faces, neither of these developments is new. Emerging markets have emerged before, and populations have aged before. None of that is unprecedented. What's different are the particular markets now in the ascendance—their profiles and how they are ascending—and a more extended aging of population than the world has hitherto seen. These facts constitute uncharted territory that we need to map if we are going to invest in it successfully.

At What Age Will We Stop Consuming?

In 1965, America's median age was 28.4 years and *declining*.[2] The trend seemed so clear that the following year, the editors of *Time* magazine proclaimed the entire generation under 25 their Man of the Year. The editors allowed as how the generation also included women, but in 1966, the times they were a-changin' somewhat slowly, and women were an afterthought. Apologies.

Time's polite sidelining of women turned out to be misguided, but the editors weren't wrong when they prophesied that the generation under 25 would "soon be the majority in charge."[3] These were the baby boomers, and as they (we) matured (or at least aged), they dictated fashion, morals, popular culture, and politics, creating what came to be called the age wave, sweeping away what had come before. But rising waves eventually crest and then fall. And that's exactly what happened here. The under-25 "majority in charge" kept getting older. By 2010, in fact, the median age of the U.S. population was 37.2, and by 2020, half of us will be 38 or older. Five years later, in 2025, 75.6 million Americans will be over the age of 60.

The pattern persists throughout most of Europe and in the wealthier countries of Eastern Asia. In 2020, for example, when our median age hits 38, the median age in China will hit 38.1, meaning that the average Chinese citizen will be slightly older than the average American. Both will seem positively youthful compared to the average Japanese, who will be pushing 50. Figure 2.1 illustrates what the population profile looks like for countries that have aged, like Japan; that *are* aging, like the United States and China; and for one country, India, that remains young. Demographers call these charts *age pyramids* because they typically show that there are fewer old people, the top of the pyramid, than young people. But now and more so in the future, those pyramids are flattening and inverting with profound implications for economies and investors.

All these projections are the inevitable consequences of a clear and unarguable demographic trend: Birthrates in the wealthy, industrialized countries of the developed world have been slowing or declining at least since the 1990s. (In the case of China, which accounts for about 20 percent of the entire world population, the declining birthrate is enforced through the one-child-per-couple law of population control.) At the same time, life expectancy has been inching forward in those countries, thanks to a general pattern of medical advances, public health care, and sophisticated lifestyle habits. It is something the world has not seen before: nations in which a rising proportion of the population consists of increasingly elderly people. If the trend continues, it could lead to something absolutely unprecedented: populations dominated by the elderly. Barring a catastrophe, the trend will continue.

What does this have to do with investing? There are at least three answers to that question. One has to do with who is eventually going to buy the assets you now own, another has to do with turning aging into profit, and the last is a caution about how age affects opportunities for the not-so-aged.

Population (in millions)

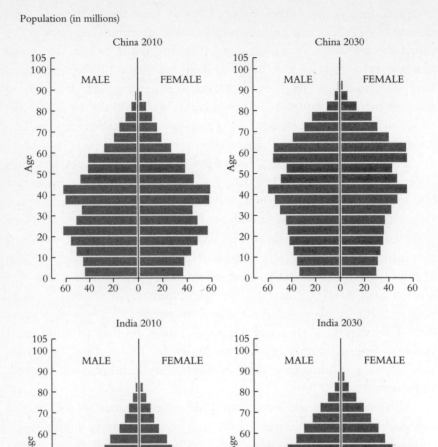

Figure 2.1 Population Profiles by Age and Sex: China, India, Japan, United States

SOURCE OF CHART DATA: United Nations, Department of Economic and Social Affairs, Population Division (2011): *World Population Prospects: The 2010 Revision* (New York); UNDP Human Development Report.

Population (in millions)

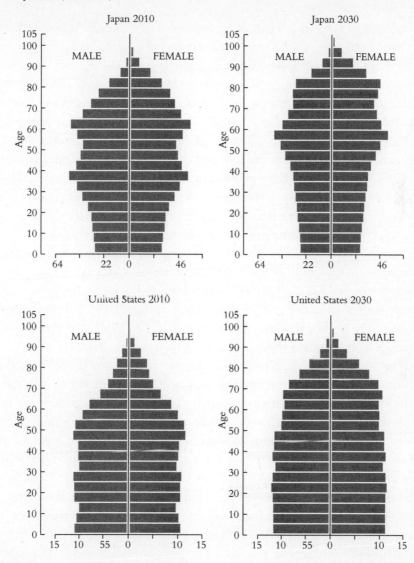

Figure 2.1 (Continued)

Age and Assets

In the summer of 2011, a pair of economists at the Federal Reserve Bank of San Francisco published a paper on the relationship between demographic trends—specifically aging—and stock prices.[4] In their paper, entitled "Boomer Retirement: Headwinds for U.S. Equity Markets?" researchers Zheng Liu and Mark Spiegel pointed out that it was baby boomers arriving at middle age, the peak years for acquiring and saving financial assets, who fueled the long and almost steady appreciation the stock market enjoyed during the Great Moderation of the 1980s and 1990s. That's neither surprising nor unusual. In fact, what happened fits the textbook standard; economists call it the life cycle view of wealth: We start out with little, accumulate more during our peak earning years, and spend it down as we age. The only difference was that there were so many boomers passing through that accumulate-and-invest period during the Great Moderation. And indeed, in their research paper, Liu and Spiegel demonstrated statistically how U.S. equity values rose along with the middle-aging of the boomers, pro-portionately more populous at the time than the elderly in the United States, as they reached their prime earning and accumulating years.

But here's the problem: The boomers are now becoming the elderly. They're at retirement age, and most are planning to sell their assets to finance that retirement; many have already begun to do so. With the demographic ratio of middle-aged to elderly declining as our overall population ages, there will be fewer peak acquirers of assets for all those retirees to sell to. To see what I mean, think of a suburb filled with classic, three-bedroom split-level houses. Once most of the 2.3 children who occupied those bedrooms have left the nest and their increasingly myopic parents get tired of tripping on the half-flight of steps, who is going to buy the houses? And if there aren't enough buyers to buy them all, what will happen to real estate prices? Nothing good. The same demographic shift could hit the stock market with similar impact. Lots of supply from retirees who are ready to sell; not so much demand: The equation does not bode well for stock prices.

That is precisely what the two Fed researchers conclude—that is, that equity values will decline as the number of sellers rises and the number of buyers doesn't, and, because markets anticipate the future, that looming imbalance can depress stock prices right now. It is a trend they believe will continue through at least 2025, when the demographics begin to shift again. At that point, although today's middle-aged asset buyers will still swell the ranks of elderly asset sellers, a new, large cohort of buyers, the so-called echo boomers, will reach their peak accumulation years. So relief is on the way—eventually. But 2025 is a long time to wait if you're planning to start selling your portfolio in the meantime.

All that sounds discouraging until we look beyond the literal and figurative borders of our investment thinking and realize that the world has changed and, for our purposes, expanded. There may be an out—an escape hatch from the trend, as the researchers themselves concede. The escape hatch leads to a population of other buyers for the assets today's retiring boomers will try to sell to dwindling ranks of middle-aged acquirers, replacement buyers who can make up the shortfall represented by our currently lopsided middle-aged/elderly demographic ratio.

Where will these other buyers come from? From well beyond U.S. borders—specifically, from the emerging-market economies[5] that are today's centers of economic growth. Their rising generation of middle-aged acquirers can swell the insufficient ranks of American middle-aged acquirers and augment the demand for that large supply of financial assets for sale, thus raising the price of stocks. Not enough Americans to buy your stock? How about letting the market find the Brazilian or the Filipino who has reached the age when newfound prosperity creates savings, and the savings start looking for investment opportunities. It makes sense, and global demand can raise the prices of the stocks as the investing life cycle reaches those far-flung populations.

There's a bit of a fly in the ointment, however. If our aging boomers are going to sell assets to a more diverse population of new investors, they will surely need to offer a more diverse portfolio of investments for sale. If we want to sell profitably, it will help to own assets others see value in buying. Doing so requires us to recognize a force in investing called the *home bias*. Do you feel more comfortable investing in a company whose name you can pronounce and whose headquarters are someplace you can visit without a passport? You probably do, and so do the Brazilians and Filipinos you'd like eventually to sell your stock to. In the next chapter, we look more closely at the perhaps less comfortable investment opportunities that businesses are creating in the emerging market and why you might want to put your own home bias aside. For now, let's simply keep in mind that we can't control the demographics of the United States and other mature economies, but we can invest around them and prosper.

Investing in Your Grandparents

There is another reason that the aging of the population affects investing, but this one's more encouraging. Simply put, the elderly represent an investing opportunity. How so? Spending power.

Again, it's all about the life cycle view of wealth, and in the case of the grandparent generation, the implications of a cohort that has pretty much stopped accumulating and is ready to spend. It's that back-end, spending-down phase that constitutes the investing opportunity. Businesses whose cash registers are well positioned to catch that spending phase stand to benefit from this advancing demographic phenomenon, and investors who identify those businesses may profit along with them.

Picture it. Imagine a place filled with retired people who, in general, enjoy good overall health and can still look forward to substantial life expectancy, have plenty of money in the bank, and have nothing to do in life except enjoy their leisure and spoil their grandchildren. Their spending—on vacations, hearing aids, restaurants, blood pressure medication, golf, and endless gifts for the grandkids at every stage of growth—represents a significant potential investment opportunity.

And here's the good news: Because such a place exists, we can get a handle on what it is like. It's called Japan, and it is the prime example, if perhaps an extreme case, of what the aging of the population can mean for investors. Japan is the oldest country in the world. During the 1966 to 2010 time period, when the U.S. median age was rising by almost nine years, from just over 28 to 37, the median age in Japan rose by more than 18 years, twice as much, from just under 27 to just over 45. By 2020, as noted, the median age in Japan will top 48.

Commentators often use those statistics to paint Japan as a country in economic decline, and there's no doubt that Japan will face a sovereign debt problem of its own in the coming years. But those demographics also define an opportunity for businesses that are alert to the implications and for investors who are alert to those businesses. While Japan is an aging country, it's also a wealthy country, and the older you are in Japan, the wealthier you are likely to be. In 2009, the median net worth of Japanese households headed by someone between the ages of 60 and 69 totaled ¥20,010,000—about $260,000—compared to overall median family net worth of ¥11,590,000, equivalent to about $150,000.[6]

Part of the explanation for that pattern of wealth is that Japan is a nation of savers—the largest creditor nation in the world—and if personal savings don't quite pay for a comfortable retirement, the accepted social contract is there to provide generous retirement pensions. Retirement age in Japan is typically around 60, and life expectancy averages out to about 83 years—a little over 79 for men and 86 for women.

So add it up: By 2025, there will be 43.6 million Japanese over the age of 60 with ample opportunity to spend their accumulated savings and pensions and with maybe some 25-plus years in which to do it. That's nearly 44 million reasons to invest in health care and leisure companies that market their goods and services in Japan.

The same phenomenon applies elsewhere. As America's baby boomers and the representatives of a similar European population bulge begin to age, they will be selling their assets to the echo boomers, their children's generation, now finally earning a living—and, they hope, to the newly prosperous of the emerging world—and they, too, will be using the proceeds to attend to their physical limitations, their prescription drugs, and Elderhostel. And while some of us are still heading to the office, flying to meet clients around the world, writing books, and hoping to continue doing so for years to come, more and more of our friends are finding that cruises and grandchildren are intellectual challenge enough. It's already happening.

Indeed, we've heard a lot of bad retirement news lately: unsustainable retirement benefits for government employees, corporate pension plans that are so underfunded that they are unlikely to meet their obligations, personal retirement accounts that won't even keep us in golf balls, and, of course, government pension plans like Social Security that promise more than they're likely to be able to deliver. I'd guess that one of the reasons you're reading this book is your concern that one of those threatened systems used to be part of your own hope for a comfortable retirement, and now you feel increasingly on your own when it comes to providing for your financial future.

The truth is, however, that for the most part, the aging population in the United States also has plenty of wherewithal. In 2009, according to the Federal Reserve Board's Survey of Consumer Finances,[7] the average American household had a net worth of $96,000—more than one-third less than the Japanese population. For those households headed by someone between the ages of 55 and 64, however, median net worth soared to $222,300, which still doesn't match the more thrifty Japanese.

Not only is the aging population growing, but despite the headlines, their wealth and spending power are substantial, and again, the businesses that recognize that spending power and the investors who recognize those businesses can prosper from the flow of cash. So for those of you worried about your retirement future, today's retirees may themselves become an opportunity; you're your own investment growth. It's another reason to honor thy father, thy mother, and all their contemporaries, and in Chapter 6 we'll take a look at how we can honor them in our portfolios.

But what is particularly profound about this aging trend is its flip side—an obvious but unwanted accompaniment to the combination of increased longevity and decreased birthrate. It's this: Economies experiencing that double whammy eventually hit a point of diminishing returns on productivity and growth. After all, how long can a country sustain a growing population of elderly—not to mention a majority population of elderly—spending down their savings but not producing anything, and dependent upon the young for a safety net of social benefits? Not that long. Growth must inevitably slow.

That is exactly what is happening in the developed world, and it is one of the most powerful reasons why the global center of economic gravity is shifting away from the developed world and toward newly emerging economies. And that is the third reason aging will affect the way you invest. A demographic reality in which the old proportionally outrank the young tells us something profound about an economy's potential for growth. That's a key signal for investors, one that not only can point us toward the opportunities in businesses that keep pace with this change but also can keep us away from businesses that will not or cannot keep pace.

The Aging Developed World and the Dependency Ratio

We hear a lot about the BRICs—Brazil, Russia, India, China—all advancing at a gallop to economic power. The populations of two of those countries, India and China, currently represent an estimated 40 percent of the population of the planet, and an awful lot of them are young and productive. Half the population of India is currently under the age of 25, and about 65 percent is somewhere below the age of 35. By the time India succeeds China as the world's most populous nation, expected around 2025 and thanks largely to China's one-child policy, the average age of an Indian will be 29; the average age of a Chinese that year will be 37, still pretty young and quite productive by most standards.

It means that these emerging markets can count on an active workforce for some time to come. It also means that for some time to come, businesses can look to these countries for both workers and customers. As investors, we must look more closely at the dynamics if we're going to identify those businesses best able to profit from this inexorable demographic shift.

The metric that tells us most about why growth in the emerging markets is speeding past the growth rate of the developed world is called the *dependency ratio*. It compares the proportion of those in a county's population who are either too young or too old to be part of the nation's labor force to the workers on whom they depend for social services, health care, education, and the like. Statisticians typically add "too young" and "too old" together, but the implications are very different. Table 2.1 reveals both a pattern of aging and a growing

Table 2.1   Median Age and Old-Age Dependency Ratios—Selected Countries, 2010

Mature Economies	Median Age (Years)	Overall Dependency Ratio*	Old–Age Dependency Ratio**
Japan	44.7	56	35
Germany	44.3	51	31
United Kingdom	39.8	51	25
United States	36.9	50	20
Australia	36.9	48	20
Emerging Economies	**Median Age (Years)**	**Overall Dependency Ratio***	**Old–Age Dependency Ratio****
India	25.1	55	8
Brazil	29.1	48	10
Turkey	28.3	48	9
China	34.5	38	11
Russia	37.9	29	19

*The overall dependency ratio is the ratio of the sum of the population aged 0–16 and that aged 65+ to the population aged 17–64. The ratio is presented as the overall number of dependents per 100 persons of working age (17–64).

**The old-age dependency ratio is the ratio of the population aged 65 years or older to the population aged 17–64. The ratio is presented as the number of old-age dependents per 100 persons of working age (17–64).

SOURCE: United Nations, Department of Economic and Social Affairs, Population Division (2011): *World Population Prospects: The 2010 Revision* (New York).

dependency issue in mature economies, but it also makes clear that we need to be cautious in generalizing this pattern.

Turkey's overall dependency ratio is higher than Japan's, but Turkey's dependents are mainly young whereas Japan's are predominantly old. Where are production facilities more likely to run at low costs? Which market is more important to a for-profit education provider? These are questions that the demographic waves push investors to ask.

In developing countries, where the birthrate tends to be high, the dependency ratio is typically a relationship between a large number of children and young people and the working-age population. This may sound like a big advantage for businesses that can sell or produce goods there, but it can be a problem. A young population means a lot of mouths for that working-age population to feed and creates the potential for discontent and disorder if those mouths face the prospect of being fed poorly. Investors are wise to be wary of the political implications. The upside, however, is that those children and youths can grow up to become productive adults who can help grow the economy. The young can grow older; if someone knows how the opposite can occur, please let me know.

In the developed world, the growing dependency problem results from the widening ranks of older people who are outside the workforce—more and more of them relative to the entire working population. With birthrates down, longevity up, and older folks increasingly unable or unwilling to continue the daily grind, many developed countries are becoming top-heavy with no-longer-working elderly supported by shrinking populations of younger, productive workers. That puts a limit on the rate at which these countries can grow, and the higher the dependency ratio of lots of old folks relying on fewer young folks, the more restrictive the limit and the slower the growth. Who wins from an investor's point of view? We'll look for companies positioned to sell the quality and value that these aging populations increasingly demand.

Again, Japan offers the most glaring example. As I write this, a 75-year-old Japanese can expect to live an average of another 14 years. That gives Japan 35 people over the age of 65 for every 100 folks between the ages of 17 and 64.

Most of Europe is in the same rocking chair. In the United States, the ratio is somewhere in between: 20 people above the age of 65 for every 100 between the ages of 17 and 64, says the United Nations' population division in its 2010 world population projections.[8] Still, any way you slice it, that's a lot of pensioners depending on fewer and fewer workers. Keep in mind that the aging trend is upward, so the situation will accelerate over time, and the growth of the affected economies will just continue to decelerate.

The emerging markets, by contrast, with their rising populations of in-their-prime workers, will still see dependency ratios fall in the years to come as their youthful populations, fueled by high birthrates, mature. India, for example, which in 2010 had 55 dependents for every 100 people of working age, will see that ratio fall to 49—38 of them too young to work—by 2025. At the same time, Japan's dependency ratio will increase to 72. Stunningly, that will mean Japan will have only two people of working age for every person over the age of 65. Now it is true that having a majority of the population in the prime age bracket for productive work is no guarantee of a nation's prosperity. But it is hard to imagine much economic growth when 72 percent of the population is out of the workforce.

What about China? Won't its repressive one-child policy create a demographic time bomb that will put it in a class with Japan for top-heavy elderly? Don't wait up. Even by 2027, China will still only have 42 dependents for every 100 workers, and only 20 of those dependents will be old. In fact, China's dependency ratio won't equal that of the United States until 2035.

But here's a comparison that really puts the color in the picture. It's pretty striking:

By 2025, the 51 percent of Indians of working age will total 744 million people, well over twice the entire American population projected for that year. By contrast, in Japan in that same year, a shrinking and aging population will have left that country with a workforce of 34.4 million, down more than 10 million from today. Again, Japan may long remain a great place in which to sell golf clubs, but the country's demographics severely limit its capacity to produce goods and services—and therefore to grow its economy.

One more development reinforces this pattern of growing labor forces in emerging economies. As they grow in number, those workers are also acquiring the skills and tools to become more productive. Figure 2.2 looks at productivity growth around the world. Despite their travails, mature economies continue to figure out how to produce more with less effort, but it's the emerging economies where productivity is booming.

Percent Change in GDP per Person Employed 1995–2010

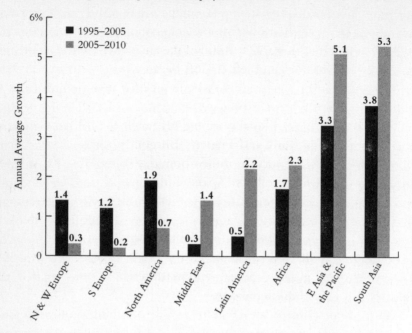

Figure 2.2 Productivity Gains in Developed and Emerging Economies

Source of chart data: The Conference Board Total Economy Database™ (www.conference-board .org/data/economydatabase), December 31, 2010. Data reproduced with permission from The Conference Board, Inc. © 2011 The Conference Board, Inc.

No wonder the center of the world's economic gravity is shifting—from the staid, increasingly superannuated, already wealthy, maybe a little tired economies of the developed world to the young, vigorous, hungry economies emerging in the developing world. As we'll see in greater detail in Chapter 4, the momentum is with them.

The Macro Factor

There is nothing abstract about these demographic shifts—the world getting older and older economies yielding to new. The investing reality they present comes with very real, very practical, very significant consequences on the ground—and they raise some questions we may not have explored before.

For example, as dependency ratios take on Japan-like proportions around the world, will health care simply eat the global economy? One has a vision of young workers fleeing economies where seven hours of their eight-hour workdays support aging pensioners and infant day care, leaving one hour for their own insufficient economic growth. Or maybe we'll get to a point where, as was said of the ancient Inuit, the elderly are just placed on ice floes and left to drift because there's no way to take care of them. Either way, it doesn't bode well for investing, unless you happen to be in the iceberg business.

On the other hand, global warming may melt the ice floes and turn Norway into a vineyard and France's Burgundy region into a Palm Springs–style desert resort. Or, if the doomsday crowd is right, we may simply run out of food, oil, and water. Either scenario would seriously upend a number of fundamental realities—sustenance, shelter, clothing— and would cause a fundamental shift in trade flows and political alliances. Right now, the world's political equilibrium, such as it is, is shaped by economics; it could work the other way around, too, with politics disaggregating the global economy and putting it back together in a way that may not bear thinking about.

Far-fetched? Doomsday scenarios usually are. Those who prophesied that the wholesale slaughter of whales in the nineteenth century would mean an eventual end to the supply of whale oil, essential for lighting and a host of other uses, were not wrong. But first came methods to extract kerosene from coal, then petroleum from drilling the earth, then electric lights and all sorts of other inventions to change the circumstances and save the whales, and the point was moot. My favorite example was an early-twentieth-century commentator who predicted that horse manure and carcasses would soon make New York unlivable. New York drivers may be getting us to the same point, but at least if you survive crossing the street, your shoes will be clean.

How are we investors supposed to deal with these what-if issues? Almost every time I meet with investors, I hear about some commentator who has figured out the *real* way the world will end—I tend to worry most about the mega-volcano under Yellowstone Park—and how that's an objection to any investment strategy we might develop today. Most of these disaster scenarios cannot be refuted, but they can be hedged. What I mean is that rather than despairing, we'll now turn to ways we can structure our portfolios to cushion the shock of these big but unlikely events. Similarly, we'll look to see how to profit from the next great opportunity we find without taking the chance of too great a loss if it disappoints.

The Bottom Line

Although financial crises and recessions are common throughout human history, our recovery from the crisis of 2007–2008 and the subsequent recession confronts us with a changed economic environment and an unfamiliar financial reality.

Familiar strategies to protect our wealth and familiar categories of asset diversification haven't worked as we'd expect them to. The sources of our current difficulties differ from our experience, and our way out must differ as well. Recovery will be protracted.

There is opportunity. While many of us focused on headline financial and economic issues, bouncing from crisis to crisis, the face of the world has been changing; in some ways and in some places, it has been changing for the better.

Major forces at work in the world have altered the financial reality the individual investor faces. Those changes will produce winners and losers. The winners will seize the opportunities created from two of the most prominent of these global shifts:

1. The shift in the economic balance of power from the developed nations to emerging economies.
2. The demographic shift embodied in the aging of the population worldwide and in the increasingly differentiated concentrations of young and of old.

With these opportunities come risks and simplistic solutions. Recognize the former and avoid the latter. Someone will always give you reason to panic. Don't.

Chapter 3

For the New Prosperity, You'll Need a New Investment Strategy

Our transformed financial landscape embraces the quotidian as well as the cosmic—the daily fluctuations of the stock market, the fall in your home value, and your neighbor's discouraging job search, as well as the rethinking of monetary policy, the resurgence of new global economic powers, and the balance between government and the private sector in growing economies.

Yes, we need to keep an eye on broad macro forces like the demographic shifts that we looked at in Chapter 2, forces beyond our control that have nevertheless drawn the outlines of a new financial reality—with implications for where, how, and in what we choose to invest.

But change has also occurred at a micro level, in the place where we actually make investment choices and pay money for them. At that level, some of the everyday assumptions we always took for granted about investing—assumptions about the way the market behaves, about debt, even about diversification—just don't work the same way anymore. They, too, have become casualties of the Great Moderation—or rather, of the investment strategy that dominated the Great Moderation. In my view, that strategy crashed and burned in the 2007–2009 financial crisis; the assumptions it gave rise to need to be put aside as well. That's what this chapter is about.

Now let me state at the outset that in explaining what I mean, I will be taking sides in a by now well-worn dispute between two schools of economic thought about how markets work. At the most basic level, the dispute is between economists who hold that the market is rational and those who hold that it is not. There is ample intellectual firepower on both sides of the argument, as there is behind the two investment strategies those points of view have generated—passive investing for those who believe the market is rational, and active investing for those who believe it is not. I hold the latter view, but in making my case I will also suggest that the situation is not quite as rigorously binary—not so exclusively either/or—as it sometimes sounds. How can we account otherwise for the fact that professional investment managers on both the passive and active sides of the dispute have achieved enormous investment wins? Similarly, both sides have suffered losses.

Like these opposing investment strategies, the current financial environment, so different from what most of us have known before, is itself not exclusively either/or. In fact, I will posit the view that there are really a lot of fine-point details about who has the strategy, resources, and market access to generate returns for investors at work in this environment, which is why investing successfully in it will require a strategy that pays attention to those details and to the subtle distinctions among them.

If we're going to take a fresh, new look at the investment strategies that can work in the world that is evolving in front of us, we need to figure out what's wrong with the strategies that have become accepted investment orthodoxy. What we'll see is that the accepted investment wisdom owes much of its success to that peculiar period of financial and economic calm that we've left behind. Let's begin, then, with an investigation of the investing strategy that held sway during the Great Moderation.

The strategy was grounded in a view of investing that holds that investigating momentous changes, like those we talked about in Chapter 2, doesn't really help much when it comes to investing.

Delving into all those macro forces—population shifts, financial crises and their aftermath, climate change, political upheaval—may make for interesting reading and may help us to understand what's going on around us, but it is irrelevant, according to this view, when it comes down to figuring out what you're going to invest in. Rather, everything you need to know about an investment is built into its price. Unless you break the law and steal information, you can't possibly know more than the vast collection of buyers and sellers who have already arrived at a price for any investment you'd consider making. As a result, you're wasting your time trying to find unrecognized opportunities to invest in or overpriced securities to sell. All an investor can do is figure out how much risk he or she is willing to take and then plug in the lowest-cost investment vehicles available to reach that level of risk. Simple as this view of investing sounds, it comes with heavyweight academic backing.

First articulated by economists at the tremendously influential University of Chicago (fun is about to die again) and known as the efficient-market hypothesis, it holds that the marketplace itself is intrinsically rational, with built-in efficiencies that ensure the greatest return for the least effort. You can't beat the market, because you can't predict what it will do or when it will do it. Analyzing how a stock has performed in the past yields only a descriptive history; it gives no clue whatsoever as to what will happen next. Trying to anticipate how shifts in world politics, demographics, and financial forces will affect the future price of a stock is a waste of time because the price already reflects more information than you'll ever be able to find and analyze yourself. Instead, the price of a stock is the only clue you have or need; it reflects every bit of information available—about past performance *and* about demographic shifts or the potential impact of global warming or a change of management at the top of the company. That constant stream of prices you can see running across the screen on your favorite television business channels represents more than people buying and selling a stock. Each price quoted embodies the world's best possible estimate of what a share of that stock is actually worth.

Since price is all you need to know, don't even bother to try to know more. Instead, investing is like taking a random walk: Your path is unpredictable, but once you've determined how much risk you're willing to take, the return you'll eventually get depends on matters of chance that you can't foresee and shouldn't attempt to anticipate. This view of investing, fueled by the efficient market hypothesis and pop-ularized in a classic book by Princeton economist Burton G. Malkiel, *A Random Walk Down Wall Street,* has been the prevailing orthodoxy in academia more or less since the 1970s.[1] The rational-market idea received an added boost and some important modifications from the new field of behavioral economics, which added an interesting gloss to the thesis early in the twenty-first century. Informed by the pioneering work of psychologist Daniel Kahneman, winner of the 2002 Nobel Prize in economics, several studies on the performance achievements of professional fund managers question whether any skill at all is involved when it comes to realizing higher returns or beating the market. Kahneman himself, in his 2011 book, *Thinking, Fast and Slow*, cites research showing zero correlation year to year in the rankings of pro-fessional fund managers. Says Kahneman, since "the consistency of individual differences in achievement" is what proves the presence of skill, this zero correlation in year-to-year performance makes any apparent superior performance appear to be a matter of sheer luck—the result of random guesswork or at best some kind of intuitive judgment. And he warns that where intuitive judgment is concerned, it's important both that the environment be "sufficiently regular to enable predictions from the available evidence" and that the professional investor has time and space to learn from his or her mistakes. It's hard to quibble with those warnings, although one might question whether zero correlation is necessarily tantamount to the primacy of sheer chance, especially since Kahneman concedes that professional investors do slightly better than individual investors.[2]

Nevertheless, the idea of the random walk through investments, bolstered by the behaviorists' questioning of long-held assumptions about how people arrive at intuitive judgments, prevailed throughout the Great Moderation; it was one reason investing was so easy during all those years. Remember? You couldn't beat the system, so you just joined it—investing in an index fund that mimicked the market or in some other form of passive-investing fund that segmented the market in a particular way. Then you sat back and watched your prosperity rise as the efficiencies of a rational market, over time, grew your wealth.

Passive was the operative word; active investing was not worth paying for. If you invested passively in an index fund, for example, you owned the same stocks in the same proportion as, for example, the Standard & Poor's (S&P) 500 index of large-cap, mostly U.S. companies (*large-cap* means large market capitalization value, which you calculate by multiplying the number of shares outstanding by the per-share stock price; in other words, the S&P 500 consists of companies with very large total market value), or the Russell 2000 index of small-cap companies, or the Dow Jones Wilshire 5000 index that tracks the entire stock market. Or maybe you invested in a passive fund focused solely on a particular slice of the market—maybe large European technology companies, or green companies, or companies with low price-to-earnings ratios. The passive part of this investing was that the fund manager just did what the index did—dropped the stocks that fell out of the index and bought the stocks that were added to it, or sold stocks that no longer fit the profile of the market slice and bought those that suddenly did. And the index did just what the market did, raising the weight of a stock as the market bid up its price, or lowering the weight as the market lost interest.

Passively allowing the market to build your portfolio is a kind of investing that is worlds away from the active investing I've done for about a quarter of a century, in which we do indeed try to read macro phenomena, stay tuned to demographic trends, follow the news about which government is up and which is down, and keep tabs on business and economic activity and what the consumer likes and dislikes. Doing that work allows us to look at individual companies; understand how adaptive a company's business strategy may be, how well it is positioned competitively, how strong its management team is, how sound its finances are, and so on; and then ask whether the market has in fact made a reasonable judgment about the price an investor should pay.

That is my experience, and it is my bias. I believe that thoughtful people can find trends in wealth creation and manage their portfolios to capture those trends—for profit. Some of those thoughtful people are quite well-known—the name Warren Buffett, of course, comes to mind, as do some of those now-famous investors who resisted the crowds flocking to U.S. mortgage debt in the middle of the last decade. But I'm thinking more of the nuts-and-bolts analysts who were early to recognize durable technological advances, the peculiarities of consumer demand in newly affluent economies, or solid companies in unglamorous industries—and to translate their analyses into financial gain.

Critics of my way of investing point out that many professional portfolio managers—maybe most, depending on the time period you pick—deliver worse returns than would the indexes, or, following the behaviorist view that it's all random luck anyway, almost never beat the market. If the professionals can't do better than an index and can't beat the market, how can *you* hope to? Or so the argument goes.

Far be it from me to question investment conclusions with quite so much intellectual power behind them, but I do suggest we ask a few questions before we follow the advice that follows from this line of thought. What I question in particular is the extent to which this kind of thinking reflects a historical period during which the rising tide of an unusually stable economic environment first lifted many boats together and then, with its sudden waning in a financial crisis, dropped them all at once. In that rising-tide environment, a successful investor only needed to board the cheapest ship and know when to disembark. In a world where economic opportunity is growing in new ways and places, investors need to take a much more differentiated look at the decisions they must make.

That is why, in my view, the rational market/passive investing strategy reads as a warning to investors: Take considerable care, it says, to understand the investment approach that lies behind any investment choice—whether it's an investment option you choose yourself or one that others select on your behalf. Perhaps the most telling insight of Kahneman and his behavioral finance followers is our all-too-human inclination to be overconfident about what we do and deny any evidence that indicates otherwise. Just as most drivers will tell you they possess above-average skill, investors—professionals included—tend to overestimate their successes and forget their mistakes. There is little doubt but that the new economic environment now evolving will produce its own set of winners and losers, and we need to think very critically about the sources of past success and the likelihood of that past success being sustained.

For all investment approaches are not equal, and investing in the post–Great Moderation world is a much more nuanced game than the random-walker academics would have you think. Once you understand that, it's clear that the pros are not as bad at doing what we do as those random-walk academics claim. For example, critics frequently point out that if you average all the mutual fund returns over most periods and compare them to index returns, the average mutual fund doesn't measure up. But of course you and I don't buy the "average" fund; we try to select funds based in an investment strategy that fits our view of how economic value is created. And we don't do such a bad job of it.

For example, by S&P's own calculation, if you weight mutual fund returns by the size of the funds producing those returns, and then compare the weighted average return with index returns, you'll find that U.S. domestic equity funds as a whole outperform the relevant S&P 1500 index.[3]

Similarly, in many investment categories, though certainly not all, investments appear to flow toward the best-performing funds. I infer from that observation that we regular folk are actually better at picking winners from among the investment options before us than the academics might think. If I'm correct, there actually is a lot to be gained from taking the time to understand and compare investment strategies. Part of my objective in explaining how I think the world of investing has changed is to help equip you to evaluate those strategies, whether you are deciding on your own what to invest in or are relying on an advisor, or maybe a fund, or someone or something else to help you decide or to make decisions for you.

Another more recent school of academic work on investing casts some further doubt on the rational-market school's conclusions about our inability to discern opportunities that the market has missed. It turns out that many active managers stick so closely to the benchmarks against which they're judged that they can't produce results that are better than those benchmarks, especially when you take fees and expenses into account. New York University finance professor Antti Petajisto calls such managers "closet indexers," and he argues that their relatively poor results skew broad averages. Professor Petajisto uses a measure he calls "active share" to identify "active stock pickers" and finds that, as a group, they do deliver market-beating investment performance.[4]

The underlying point of this book is my conviction that the kind of work I do can help you prosper from the changed world we're all living in now—as long as you first understand the change. You and I will do the work together as we go through each chapter. We will analyze the change and then, within that understanding, identify a range of different actions—of vehicles and prices—from among which you can make choices. These choices will work with your personal proclivities, values, and investment goals. But I believe fervently that the more knowledge you have gleaned and the sharper the insights you have gained, the more you will profit from the choices you make. In the old saying, "investigate before you invest." This book is giving you questions to ask in that investigation.

Looking for Help in Building an Investment Plan

Throughout this book, I make it clear that structuring a durable and effective investment portfolio is neither easy nor quick nor a one-shot operation. Finding some professional help is a reasonable next step. If you decide to use a planner for some or all of your needs, there are a few things to keep in mind. First, if he or she lets you get away with ignoring your investment statements except when you know they're going to look good, consider finding someone else. You need to be informed, and you need an advisor who wants you to be informed.

Most of us start with recommendations from someone we trust, but listen for the recommendation that says, "This planner made me think about things I hadn't considered," rather than the recommendation that says, "This guy's making me a killing." Interview several prospects and watch for someone who begins by asking you to discuss the liability side of your plan, your responsibilities, and your aspirations before launching into a discussion of investment strategies. You both must know what you'll need before you start figuring out how to get there.

Some advisors offer one-stop shopping for planning, investment, estate, and even tax advice; some specialize and provide referrals to specialists in other fields. The more complicated your plan, the more you may require one or more specialists. Clarify as you interview, and score points for the person who knows what he or she doesn't know.

And speaking of knowledge, use this book to test how aware a potential advisor is about how and why the world has changed and is changing. Can your advisor candidate get beyond the headlines about China or the current political scene and talk sensibly about consequent threats and opportunities in your financial plan? You're not looking for an economist; you want a practitioner, but you want to avoid someone who is stuck in the old solutions just as you'll want to avoid someone who has no idea what came before the current set of circumstances. Perspective will prove valuable as conditions and circumstances continue to change.

Be wary if specific packaged products come up too soon and too frequently in the conversation, and know how your advisor gets paid. An advisor who helps you get a financial plan on track should be fairly compensated, whether through fees or commissions, but he or she should be fully open about how that compensation works and where compensation could influence recommendations. You should both want compensation to be discussed because a successful relationship requires trust, and as the saying goes, "Trust, but verify." After all, when you see the doctor you at least get one of those gowns that covers you up pretty well—provided you take tiny, mincing steps down the clinic corridor. With your financial advisor, you're fully exposed. And speaking of trust, you may want to visit the Financial Industry Regulatory Authority (FINRA) website (www.finra.org); there, among other things, you can check out a prospective advisor's regulatory record.

However thorough, effective, and trustworthy the planner you choose turns out to be, stay involved. After all, even if no major changes take place in your life, your situation changes every 12 months just because your planning horizons draw closer by a year. Plans need to be a source of stability in your finances, but they must not be static. Finally, financial planning, especially its investment side, can and should be an opportunity to learn, expand your horizons, and test ideas on other thoughtful people. Don't miss out.

How the Random-Walk Orthodoxy Lost Its Way

You might dismiss my view as an example of "where you stand depends on where you sit," and admittedly, I sit at a desk in a large Wall Street investment firm. But I just don't believe, in Burton Malkiel's classic phrase, that "a blindfolded chimpanzee throwing darts at the stock listings can select a portfolio that performs as well" as one you actively manage—not in today's changed world, anyway. Neither will an index fund that relies on the rationality of the market, the preferred investment vehicle of the random-walk proponents. Here's why:

For one thing, the purity of this concept of the rational market as the determining factor in passive index investing is something of a fallacy. Almost by definition, the collection of securities into an index fund is an attempt to represent an economic reality that cannot be fully captured. The market may or not be rational, but the attempt to replicate it in an index fund is arbitrary. Just like actively managed funds, a passively managed fund that seeks to replicate an index of securities and produce the same returns as the index is a human construction. Somebody—or a committee of somebodies—decides which sector of the market to track to create the index; determines the calculation for weighting potential entrants into the index; selects the stocks, bonds, or commodities to be included; kicks out those that no longer fit; and adds others that do. Investing in a passively managed index fund is a lot less like watching a chimpanzee throw darts than it is like buying a box of cereal: You need to read the label carefully to understand the ingredients. The committee that manages the S&P 500 index, for example, tries to achieve a balance among industry sectors and to avoid companies whose equities are relatively illiquid. It also changes the index to reflect changes in market capitalization. Investing in an S&P index fund, therefore, isn't exactly tantamount to being blithely driven by the pure rationality of the market.

Moreover, as index funds become more specialized, they also become less representative of the market segment they try to replicate. Bond market indexes may include thousands of securities. Funds that try to mimic those indexes can't own all the bonds in the index and therefore use statistical models to try to achieve similar returns. Those returns sometimes deviate significantly from the targeted index's returns.

The same thing happens with commodity index funds. Since fund managers can't keep cattle and pigs on the premises, or grow corn in their offices, or store sheets of aluminum in the hallways, such funds will typically own derivatives—futures and options contracts—in order to replicate the market prices of cattle, pigs, corn, and aluminum. Again, returns from the derivatives may deviate from the prices of the commodities themselves, and investors may end up with investment returns that don't live up to their expectations.

And that's only for creating a passive index fund. What worries me most about passive index investing is how, once the fund is up and running, it forces investors to follow the crowd. According to Wharton economist Jeremy Siegel, in fact, the requirement that indexes replicate current market weights in assembling a portfolio of stocks actually tends to harm investors' returns.[5] Because the managers try to do just what the market is doing, index funds tend to swing this way and that as the market swings, going to the same extremes, one way and another, that the market goes to. In the middle years of the past decade, for example, when the financial sector was creating lots of leverage and lots of profits and financial companies were the darlings of the U.S. stock market, indexes, which are usually calculated by market capitalization, tended to be weighted heavily in financials. By 2007, for example, nearly 30 percent of the market weight of the S&P 500 was in financial institutions. Goldman Sachs, Citigroup, Lehman Brothers, Bear Stearns, American International Group (AIG), Bank of America—all the great names of the financial world were there in 2007, providing investors in S&P 500 index funds nearly 30 percent of their earnings.

That turned out to be not such a good idea the following year, when Lehman Brothers and Bear Stearns went belly-up and the sell-off of financial stocks had become a torrent. That's when those who passively follow the market followed it right over the cliff of the financial crisis. Nor was the 2007 disaster an isolated occurrence. Siegel uses the tech wreck of the early 2000s to illustrate the risk investors take on when, in an attempt to be neutral, they follow the market into whatever is hot at the moment.[6]

Of course, we cannot know how many financial stocks Malkiel's blindfolded chimpanzee would have hit and what the results would have been. It must also be assumed that the lemmings running over the cliff in both the tech wreck and the 2007 meltdown included many active managers and individual investors. But someone actively managing a portfolio at least had a shot at ensuring that the portfolio was not as heavily weighted in the financial sector as the S&P 500 was just before it took a deep, deep downward dive.

In a very real sense, it comes down to what you want to own. Passive investing in index funds decides that for you, attributing the decision to the putative inherent efficiency of a rational market's invisible hand, and then ties *your* hands. That may not have mattered so much during the Great Moderation, but in today's highly volatile markets, it's a reason for concern and caution.

Don't get me wrong: I believe there is a place for index funds; they can play an important role in a portfolio. In fact, if you promise not to tell my employer, I'll admit that I own some index funds. They can be especially useful when you decide to allocate funds to a market segment but need time to decide on a more selective approach and want to benefit from the potential appreciation of the overall market. Index-based investments also serve well when you want to follow a general investment philosophy about value and opportunity, rather than feel yourself tied to a specific company, debt issuer, or portfolio management style. For example, some investment strategies you'll hear about might lead you to decide that a single factor, such as a company's stock price compared to its book value, its pace of earnings growth, its history of dividend payment, or its market price pattern, is all you need to know about a successful investment. Though I'm skeptical about such simplistic strategies, you probably can find an index-based vehicle for investing in a broad sample of representative companies that addresses your strategy. But, again, I'm skeptical.

In short, we can give Professor Malkiel's chimpanzee a little help with his aim. Back to my cereal box analogy. Since it turns out that no fund's ingredients are exactly random, and even the supposedly nutritious brands can contain a bit more sugar and a bit less fiber than we might like, reading the label might be good for your financial health. Price isn't the only thing that matters. But in general, the orthodoxy of the rational market has quite rightly become a casualty of the financial crisis and its hangover.

There's another reason the old orthodoxy needs a fresh look. Think of it as a grace note from the emerging markets. Remember the study discussed in Chapter 2 about America's boomers not finding enough buyers for the stocks they need to sell to fund their retirement—and the threat that poses to equity values? One way out of the bind, the authors suggested, could be the rising middle classes of the emerging markets. They can be the buyers of those equity portfolios, and their demand for same can keep stock prices from plummeting. The fly in the ointment that I mentioned is that the boomers' equity portfolios need to include the stocks that Brazilians, Russians, Indians, and Chinese will *want* to buy over the next 15 or 20 years.

As it happens, however, Brazilians, Russians, Indians, and Chinese, just like the rest of us, show a strong if irrational preference for investing in companies headquartered in their own countries. How do you factor irrational human behavior into rational market forces? With some careful work I'll give you some direction on in the next chapter, you might identify some of Brazil's future market stars. But you're certainly not going to find them in a domestic American index fund. You may have a better chance of catching them in an index of emerging-market stocks, but there's a problem with emerging-market indexes, as we'll see a bit later.

Remember that the Great Moderation worked because policy makers, especially central bankers like the Federal Reserve, had figured out how to ease and tighten credit and keep the economy and financial markets on an even keel. When the sailing is that smooth, you can ride on just about anything that floats and get where you want to go. But when rough seas are the result not of a passing storm but of a fundamental economic climate change, investors need to be much more careful about which ship they board. In other words, the set-it-and-forget-it investment strategy of the Great Moderation is as cold as the Great Moderation itself. Random walking—or random sailing—won't get you very far. Profiting from what you can't change is going to take some effort.

Looking for Safety

For a goodly number of investors, safety has become the new investment strategy. Rather than board any ship at all, these investors have reacted to all the turmoil by deciding to stay put on dry land—to preserve what they have rather than take the chance of further losses in the pursuit of gain.

The result of this rush to perceived safety is that huge amounts of money have been channeled into bond funds and varieties of bank deposits. The Investment Company Institute reported that between 2008 and 2010, U.S. investors withdrew $279.9 billion from equity funds and added $645 billion to bond funds.[7]

That's quite a switch, and it makes quite a statement, especially when we recall that bonds were a financial orphan during the Great Moderation, even though inflation remained steady and low, and even though credit problems were largely restricted to an occasional spasm in the high-yield junk bond market. I recall from the latter half of the 1990s the loneliness of the fixed-income portfolio manager. At my firm's monthly conferences for financial advisors, my assignment was to wow the audience with the many attractions of the bond market. It took me a while to figure out why my speaking time was right after lunch:

everyone would be asleep anyway. Now, however, thanks to investors' pursuit of safety, to massive Fed bond purchases, and to foreign countries building up huge treasure troves of U.S. government debt, U.S. Treasury securities' interest rates are very low—so low that interest payments don't keep up with inflation. And, since bond prices rise as interest rates fall, government bonds have provided one of the rare sources of principal gains through the recent market turmoil. Rock-bottom interest rates may be fine for the government, but what about those of us looking for a good, safe mattress to stuff our money under? Bonds, U.S. Treasury bonds at least, may not be the shelter they have been. In Chapter 7, we'll look in detail at what bonds can and cannot do to improve your portfolio's performance. But for now, suffice it to say that if people are paying more attention to bond managers these days, we'd better be on guard.

Remember, we're thinking about investment success in terms of future purchasing power. From an investor's point of view, it makes little difference why an investment's return buys less in the future—whether because the prices of the things we purchase have outstripped an investment's returns or because the investment has lost market value. What matters is the loss. In a way, interest rates that don't keep up with inflation—negative real interest rates in the jargon of economists—are worse than market uncertainty. After all, no matter how disappointing today's market prices may be, markets can reverse themselves, and you may eventually be able to sell an investment at a gain that beats the rise in the cost of living. When, however, you accept a negative real interest rate, a rate that means that each coupon payment buys less than did the one before, you can be sure that you're losing purchasing power. And when you lose purchasing power, you lose standard of living as well—not what you aim for when you invest.

Is this negative real interest rate problem a passing phenomenon or is it another feature of our new economic environment? I tend to think it's the latter. Some would even argue that the Fed is intentionally keeping Treasury rates below the rate of inflation in an effort to help reduce the burden of federal debt. The reason? If the government can continue to borrow at low cost and then repay its debts in cheaper and cheaper dollars, it can ease the public debt problem without daring the more painful alternatives of sharply reduced spending or higher taxes—a strategy some economists have called "financial repression."[8] Good news for bondholders? After all, rates would remain low and prices high.

Hardly. Cheaper and cheaper dollars eventually mean higher and higher inflation, and eventually the bond market will respond with higher yields and lower prices. So if today's low rates are a temporary aberration, bond investors' problems are doubled because as rather pitiful rates rise, today's low-interest-rate securities will lose value in the market.

Again, the reason may not matter. What matters is that it's time to give up the old assumption about where to find safety from the volatility of the market.

Even Diversification?

Yup. Even the simple approach to diversification advanced by the old orthodoxy has become a casualty of our transformed financial landscape—deservedly so. Note that I do not say diversification has to go. On the contrary. It remains one of the most powerful tools available to investors. Rather, it's the way it has been applied—as a hammer rather than a screwdriver—that needs to be put aside if diversification is to achieve its very, very important purpose in the post–Great Moderation era.

It isn't for nothing, after all, that financial economists who have focused on diversification have received Nobel Prizes; the theory works. Basically, what it says is that if some investments dependably appreciate at the same time that others decline—that is, some zig while others zag—a portfolio that contains both ziggers and zaggers lets you smooth out the overall portfolio's volatility, reducing its total risk. The jargon is that such a portfolio has weak—or better yet, negative—intercorrelations among its holdings; that is, the investments within the portfolio don't tend to have the same price action at the same time. While the prices of some investments in the portfolio may be rising, the prices of others will be falling, so the good performance of the ziggers will offset the bad performance of the zaggers. Such a portfolio won't match the returns of the best individual holding, but it won't match the losses of the worst holding, either. It'll give you the average return but less than the average volatility—not a bad deal in an increasingly volatile world.

Using it as we did during the Great Moderation, however, won't work anymore—applying the hammer blow rather than the nuanced adjustment of a screwdriver. Back then, for example, an investor could achieve diversification by balancing a domestic portfolio with international stocks and bonds. The world was less globalized then, and a company's economic prospects depended more heavily on its home country's business cycle, which tended to be quite different from another country's business cycle. For example, when the U.S. stock market crash of October 1987 left the S&P 500 with a modest price increase of 2 percent for the year, the still-soaring Japanese Nikkei index weathered the storm much better, returning more than 14.5 percent for the year. And when recession-plagued 1990 saw an almost 40 percent decline in the Nikkei, the S&P 500, supported by the Great Moderation, lost a much less jarring 6.5 percent—only a 3.1 percent decline if you include dividends. So the investor could readily diversify performance in a portfolio just by mixing up companies' bases of operation—adding stocks of companies based in a few different locations.

In the post–Great Moderation reality, however, building a diversified portfolio has become more complicated and requires careful fine-tuning, not a wallop over the head. Today, as companies large and small increasingly depend on selling in markets far from home, their fortunes depend on economic developments beyond their own borders. Those developments can conceivably wipe out the diversification advantage mere location once achieved. The difference between the business cycle in, say, Malaysia and that in Peru was once significant enough—and the correlations between companies based in the two different locations weak enough—that you could diversify a portfolio by investing in both. Now, however, indexes of domestic and international stocks and bonds are zigging and zagging in unison.[9] Portfolios that once contained minimal intercorrelations are now marching in lockstep; they require the torque adjustment of a screwdriver to unlock the connections and spread the risk of volatility. The old, easy paths to diversification by hammer can now lead to big trouble.

But maybe you're not particularly worried about volatility. You're in for the long haul; you plan to hold on to your investments and can ride out the zigs and zags; you want to concentrate your money on what you consider your very best ideas. That's a fair point. It makes for prudent investing, and I focus on the long term as well, but before you decide to ignore volatility as a criterion for your investment decisions, let me tell you about my basement. While I was busy writing this book, Hurricane Irene dumped about two feet of water into my basement, and before I could even begin to calculate the damage, my insurance company sent me a letter quoting my policy's recent amendment excluding exactly such a peril. Whatever fixing the flood damage might cost, I was on my own to come up with the cash. From a financial planning perspective, a portion of my investment horizon changed from years to days as I produced the cash to pay for repairs. So much for long-term investing. Here's where volatility plays a role. If all I had owned was my one brilliant but volatile investment idea, and if it so happened that the financial storm that accompanied Irene had depressed the market's appetite for my brilliant idea, I would have been forced to liquidate the investment at a lousy price. Fortunately, I'd held some cash back from my better ideas and could pay for the damage and wait for a better opportunity to rebalance my portfolio.

So let me suggest that when you finish this chapter, you please go reread your insurance policies. Meanwhile, take it from me that volatility is something to consider very carefully in devising a new investment strategy for the post–Great Moderation era. The chapters that follow will offer ways to come up with good, very good, maybe even brilliant investment ideas, but even in a portfolio full of sensational ideas, you'll need to make sure they don't all zig or zag at same time. To do so, it's important to return to some basics: Investment Strategy 101.

Your New Investment Strategy

So you've put some old assumptions to rest. You've cleansed your mind of the random-walk orthodoxy of the past and its unquestioning embrace of the passive index fund. You've cautioned yourself about where to look for safety, and you've looked anew at how to use diversification as a tool of investing. You're left with a clean slate on which to build a new investment strategy that will help you profit from the new reality.

Perhaps the first step is to accept a fairly universal old reality—namely, that the likelihood that you will stumble upon the totally undiscovered Next Big Thing and make a killing on it is remote at best. Instead of looking for the next Apple available at (a split-adjusted) $2.82 a share and appreciating by over 166 times, you're far better off searching for a quiverful of companies selling for $20 a share that have a good chance of appreciating to $60 a share.

The trick, of course, is to know those companies when you see them. To do that, it's helpful to remember what we all too often forget: how investing makes us money. Because stock markets seem to take on a life of their own, we can sometimes forget that there really is an economic reality behind those numbers flashing across the electronic ticker, and however exciting the gyrations of the flashing numbers may be, we ignore that underlying reality at our peril.

The economic reality starts when somebody gets a great idea for a moneymaking enterprise. Unless she has at hand all the resources she needs to hire workers, buy machinery, and set up a distribution system, she will require investors. And she will come looking for them—for you—in the capital markets. There, in exchange for capital to get going on her idea, she'll offer you one of two propositions: the bondholder proposition or the shareholder proposition.

In the bondholder proposition, in exchange for the capital you give her, she will pay you periodically for the use of the capital and will give it back to you at a fixed time in the future. You've simply joined a group of investors collectively making a loan, and once the loan is paid back, that's it. You knew ahead of time what you were going to earn, and now that you've got it, you're quits.

In the shareholder proposition, the woman with the moneymaking idea effectively makes you a partner in the business by offering you, in exchange for the capital you put up, a share of her earnings in perpetuity. Unlike the bondholder, you as shareholder do not know the return in advance. Instead, you're betting that the profits will exceed expectations. You make that bet because you believe there is value in the idea and a potential for growth that the world at large—and other investors—have missed or underestimated.

The more the world doubts the idea, the sweeter the incentive the idea-innovator will offer to lure you aboard. She'll raise the rate of interest she offers the bondholder or lower the price of shares she will sell to a shareholder. For both bondholders and shareholders, it's a chance to stand apart from the crowd and have a shot at something a lot better than crowd-like returns. But it is also risky; if the world was right and you're wrong, you lose.

This perspective also shapes the way we think about diversification. We'll consider the issue in more detail in Chapter 9, but there's an important point to be made here. When we look for diversification, we'll be looking to diversify the economic strengths of the investments we make, not just their easily measurable characteristics. Traditional diversification methods would, for example, applaud your offsetting a consumer goods company in your portfolio with a transportation provider. That sounds right, and it's easy to measure. But what if most of the customers for the first company's toothpaste are the same people as the passengers on the other company's airline? And what if those customers and passengers all live someplace with rising unemployment? It turns out your portfolio isn't as diversified as it might have been had you owned two airlines serving two different passenger bases. We want our good ideas to be based on differing sources of value and growth, not on easy but misleading classifications. That way, if one source of growth— say, access to rapidly growing consumer markets—falls out of favor, another—say, access to well-off retirees—might replace it.

In sum, your strategy must be to find the ideas that will exceed expectations in the current totally changed financial reality and to diversify the economic logic of those ideas. It's not easy, but it's also not as hard as it sounds. In much of the rest of this book, we'll look in detail at where and how we can find those ideas. Let's begin with a brief categorization of what they likely entail.

What Do Good Ideas Look Like?

The characteristics of good moneymaking ideas are pretty much the same as they always were; it's identifying these characteristics in a context unlike any we've ever seen before that is the tough part. You might find the engineering arcane, the location of operations unfamiliar, and the principals' names unpronounceable. Still, you look for the distinctions that can make a difference—of technological prowess, branding, market access, even productivity.

Technology

A good idea in technology does something that people want done or can be convinced they want done and that nobody else can do—at least not yet or not as well or not as cheaply. When I suggested that you should not be looking for the next Apple, I meant that you should not fantasize that you are going to find one of history's most successful companies in the garage next door. But certainly, the kind of vision that made Apple great—and that Apple has further stimulated—is out there and worth looking for.

Technologies increasingly define the way we live and are profoundly changing classic business models in manufacturing, service, entertainment, journalism, and commerce; even in the writing, reading, and publishing of books; and certainly in medicine and health care. Process and product innovations in orthopedic implants, for example— new knees, hips, and spines—have made this a multibillion-dollar market; the beauty part is that it serves two growing demographic segments: one, the brittle-boned aging population, and two, the active-lifestyle 20-, 30-, and 40-something joggers and gym-goers, heli-skiers, and speed-hikers—the weekend warriors proving their mettle in ever more extreme sports.

The possibilities for technological innovation are limitless, and yes, there is a lot of junk and a fair amount of hype along with the successes. Many of us remember the dot-com mania of the late 1990s and the irrational response investors had to it. But building a better mousetrap has always been a good way to make money, and in a very high-tech world, it still is.

Branding

If you build it, they may come, but when they do, they're likely to be wearing North Face jackets and Ugg boots and to be protecting their iPads (Apple again!) with SmartCovers. It isn't just that people want to use these products; rather, they ask these products to speak for them. The product endows them with an image or a style they can aspire to and to which they want to belong. The right brand carries the promise of quality, prestige, and status. Once established, powerful brands acquire staying power, and they acquire pricing power for the companies that produce them. Investors should weigh brand power heavily in their analysis—and remain alert to the fading allure. Remember when Buick was a prestige brand?

Market Access

When we talked about the world's changing demographics, by implication we were also talking about the world's changing markets. Whether your product is a sure winner for the growing crop of the aging in developed economies or will be the next must-have for the burgeoning middle class in emerging ones, it's all for naught until you can get your product to the market and into buyers' hands. Walk through an Indian street market, and you'll see small packages of Western-brand laundry detergent hanging from vendors' gates. Small shops, small homes, and small budgets don't invite large, economy-sized boxes of laundry detergent. The companies that understand demand in this way are the ones that will profit from the changing world of demand. Success in reaching new and growing markets means running the gauntlet of legal, cultural, logistical, and linguistic challenges. The greater a market's potential, the greater those challenges are likely to be. The company that can reach those markets as they want to be reached will see sustainable profits. Investors need to figure out what company that is.

Productivity

You're not necessarily building a better mousetrap; rather, you're building the classic mousetrap better and more cheaply. You're cutting costs, outsourcing a range of back-office functions, or focusing on efficiencies, and are therefore able to provide a standard product that is widely needed at a lower price in order to realize a higher profit margin. How else do you explain the global success of the highly efficient large-scale retailers like Carrefour and Walmart, and the vigor with which small competitors fight them off in places as different as Japan and India? You may not maintain that competitive edge forever or even for very long, and your investors had better be vigilant. But while the productivity edge lasts, it's a moneymaker.

The Price of Opportunity

None of this matters if you overpay. Even if markets aren't perfect and do leave opportunities for thoughtful investors, markets are pretty smart and tend to price investments somewhat efficiently. They also tend to price the most exciting ideas expensively. So caution is in order, especially when there's a buzz. If everyone thinks something is a great investment idea, it probably once was.

So now all you have to do is find, within the context of shifting centers of economic activity and transformative demographics, the businesses that demonstrate these characteristics and that are starved for capital. It's a good bet that those businesses are where the wealth is, and that's the place to go next.

The Bottom Line

The macro changes in the world's financial reality require an accompanying change in the day-to-day approach to investing. The financial crisis challenged the long-accepted orthodoxy of a rational, efficient market and found it wanting in the new, post–Great Moderation financial reality. As others cling to old solutions or simply run for cover, the opportunity has grown to profit from the shifting profile of economic growth.

Investors need to look closely at the strategies embedded in both active and passive approaches to investing in the new environment, especially because seemingly passive vehicles contain assumptions and biases of their own. Active management of our investment portfolios can produce favorable results, whether we do it ourselves or find effective managers to guide us.

Whichever path you choose, there is considerable homework to be done. The post–Great Moderation reality challenges the traditional safe haven of investing—bonds—which are no longer the shelter they once were. The traditional approach to diversification depended on overly simplified asset categories and largely failed us in recent years.

The future of developing a diversified investment portfolio demands that we look more closely for differentiated sources of economic value, not just at simplistic categories of assets.

Bottom line: A more nuanced investment strategy is required. Finding it starts with redefining how economic value can be created and sustained in the new reality.

Chapter 4

Where the Wealth Is

S ay "Brazil" and what comes to mind? Dancing to the bossa nova and 50 percent inflation.

What do you think of when you think of Indonesia? A spicy *nasi goreng*, and military rule.

Keep the bossa nova and the *nasi goreng*, and then think again. Both countries are among the fastest-growing economies in the world. As of this writing, Indonesia's growth rate is more than twice that of the United States, and Brazil's is almost three times greater. These countries, and anywhere from 15 to 40 others, depending on which list you favor, constitute today's emerging markets. They are countries we didn't used to think of as economic powerhouses or investing opportunities, which is why I suggested that disenthralling ourselves of old perceptions was the first step toward investing successfully in a world we can't change.

The Emerging World Emerges—Fast

The term *emerging market* (EM) risks obscuring as much as it describes; in fact, it may already be outliving its usefulness. That's not surprising; so did the series of terms that preceded it—underdeveloped, less developed, third world—and so, eventually, will more current terms like growth markets. What counts, however, and what is at issue here, is the economic process wherever and however fast it occurs. That process— and my definition, therefore, of an EM country—is an economy that is moving from subsistence to industrialization and from labor arbitrage to capital-intensive manufacture as its people rise from poverty into a newly forming middle class. The point of the definition is to distinguish between economies that are undergoing that process and those, primarily in the North Atlantic region, Oceania, and Japan, where that socioeconomic transformation has long since largely occurred.[1]

In today's emerging-market economies, that transforming process has been rapid in pace, especially when measured against the past. Consider the time line in Figure 4.1. In Italy at the dawn of the Renaissance, in that midpoint of the fifteenth century when all those

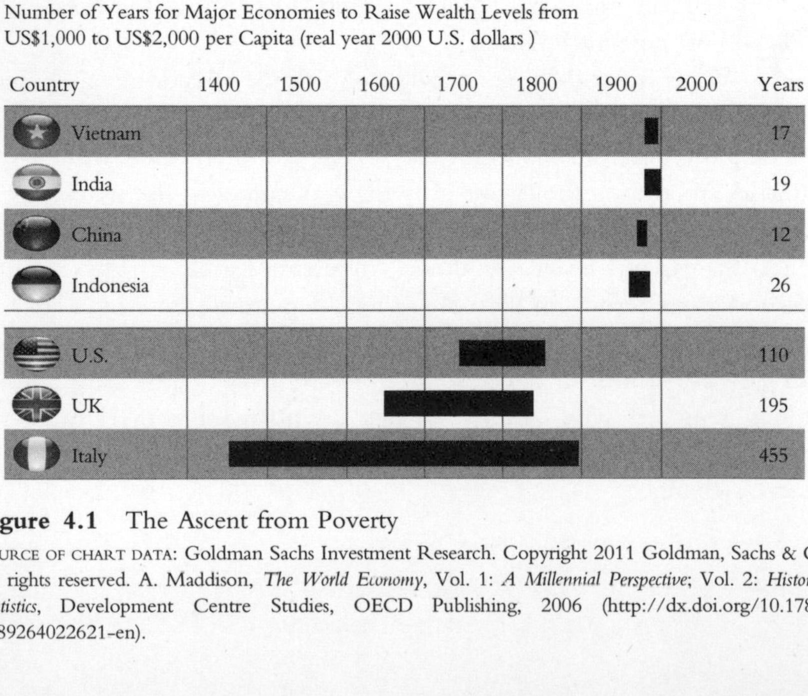

Number of Years for Major Economies to Raise Wealth Levels from
US$1,000 to US$2,000 per Capita (real year 2000 U.S. dollars)

Country	1400	1500	1600	1700	1800	1900	2000	Years
Vietnam								17
India								19
China								12
Indonesia								26
U.S.								110
UK								195
Italy								455

Figure 4.1   The Ascent from Poverty

Source of chart data: Goldman Sachs Investment Research. Copyright 2011 Goldman, Sachs & Co. All rights reserved. A. Maddison, *The World Economy*, Vol. 1: *A Millennial Perspective*; Vol. 2: *Historical Statistics*, Development Centre Studies, OECD Publishing, 2006 (http://dx.doi.org/10.1787/9789264022621-en).

extraordinary artists were creating all those extraordinary works of art, the level of wealth, expressed in current U.S. dollars, was $1,000 per capita. It took 455 years, until around the year 1900, for the Italian economy to double that wealth level to $2,000 per capita, the level at which a country can be thought of as middle-income.

A bit later, it took Britain much less time to effect the same transition—only about 195 years, from 1650 to around 1845.

And it took the United States even less time—just a little over a century, from the time of the French and Indian War to the time of the Civil War, circa 1750 to 1850 or so—to achieve that rise from poverty.

India, Indonesia, and Vietnam, however, have made the same leap from poverty in 19, 26, and 17 years, respectively. And China did it in only 12 years.[2]

The speed of this transformation means that as of this writing, 40 percent of the world's population is rapidly leaving poverty behind. People who live in countries we have heretofore thought of as exotic adventure-travel destinations, if we thought about them at all—people we typically picture in our minds as subsistence farmers or day laborers— are actively rewriting the script we have for them.

The new script is not written solely in dollars and cents. For all the nations emerging out of poverty, the consequences of market growth are felt also in advances in life expectancy, literacy, and education, and sometimes even in rising levels of equality, security, and environmental protection—in other words, in overall quality of life. These are the indicators the United Nations measures in assessing human development around the world, and the UN's Human Development Index (HDI), which tracks the change in human development country by country and over the years, makes it pretty clear that the EM countries are seeing substantive upward development in their rate of advancement compared to that of the wealthy developed nations. From the remarkable changes shown in Table 4.1, you see how rapid progress has been, but we also should recognize (and here's the opportunity) how much is left to accomplish.

Certainly, building an integrated global economy by developing human capital—a fancy way of saying that people learn to do economically valuable things—is all to the good. And the two forces, global integration and economic development, for the most part go hand in hand. That is, as people grow richer, healthier, and better educated in

Table 4.1 Emerging Markets: Rising GDP Means Rising HDI

Country	% Change in GDP per Capita 1990–2010	% Change in HDI 1990–2010	Country	% Change in GDP per Capita 1990–2010	% Change in HDI 1990–2010
Brazil*	39.6%	—	Canada	33.8%	5.1%
Chile	107.4%	16.0%	France	26.0%	13.8%
China	505.5%	44.1%	Germany	19.5%	8.6%
Colombia	37.6%	19.0%	Italy	28.8%	13.2%
Czech			Japan	14.3%	11.8%
Republic*	41.0%	—	United		
Egypt	69.4%	28.1%	Kingdom	39.5%	10.3%
Hungary	39.6%	16.3%	United States	34.9%	5.3%
India	156.4%	33.4%			
Indonesia	94.4%	31.0%			
Korea	137.5%	21.0%			
(South)					
Malaysia	100.3%	20.8%			
Mexico	29.3%	18.1%			
Morocco	59.6%	34.7%			
Peru	86.8%	18.9%			
Philippines	39.5%	15.6%			
Poland	114.1%	16.4%			
Russia	15.0%	3.9%			
South Africa	19.7%	−0.7%			
Taiwan**	128.80%	—			
Thailand	94.2%	19.8%			
Turkey	52.2%	23.0%			

*A Human Development Index was not calculated in 1990 for Brazil or the Czech Republic.
**A separate HDI is not calculated for Taiwan.
SOURCE: National Statistics, Republic of China (Taiwan), http://eng.stat.gov.tw/ct.asp?xItem=25763&CtNode=5347&mp=5; United Nations, Human Development Report Office, "International Human Development Indicators," http://hdrstats.undp.org/en/tables/default.html.

one place, those developments spread outward, and other people elsewhere participate in the process of growing richer, healthier, and better educated. China's extraordinary economic growth, for example, has spilled over to spur growth throughout Southeast Asia and even Latin America; it has also challenged such laggards as India and, arguably, the United States. For investors, it's important to understand the engines that drive that process before we take a look, in the next chapter, at how to approach investing in emerging-market countries.

What's Driving the Emergence of the Emerging Markets?

The modern world's first great wave of globalization got going as the Industrial Revolution of the eighteenth century and the Pax Britannica of the nineteenth allowed trade to fan out from the North Atlantic powers to reach markets around the world. Even forcibly colonized markets felt the reach of this expansion, and they grew and developed, whether they liked it or not. Peace reigned—most of the time, and on the great powers' home territory, anyway; production and commerce flourished; growth was sustained and unprecedented; and just about every aspect of daily life improved, at least for the owning classes in the industrial nations. The century between Napoleon's fall in 1815 and the outbreak of World War I in 1914 saw advances in transportation, communication, production, and finance that rival our own recent history and that definitely changed the world.

And new markets emerged. Preeminent among them was the United States, which grew from a colonial backwater to the world's largest economy. Countries like Japan, Canada, Australia, and Argentina joined the growth party. China, by contrast, the world's largest economy at the end of the eighteenth century, stagnated in its own civil discord and under the weight of foreign invasion and regressed economically. China's nineteenth-century decline and twentieth-century turmoil make its emergence today, following two centuries of slack and misery, even more stunning.

As with the global economic wave that was building 200 years ago, today's economic tide owes its strength to the confluence of technological, financial, and political forces. The surge of global trade in the nineteenth century was propelled by the transformation from sail to steam transportation. Today, while many of the world's goods still move at steamship speed, information travels at the speed of light. Even speedier, it seems, is the pace of advancement: In 1990, the number of people worldwide with their own Internet access was 2.6 million; by 2009, users totaled 1.8 billion.[3] As you know, the number keeps on rising.

This also changes the world, profoundly. In 1974, when I was living in Lyon, France, gathering data for my doctoral dissertation, French postal workers went on strike, leaving my monthly research stipend marooned in some mail-sorting facility somewhere in France. Since telephone operators faced the same class enemy and had staged a sympathy strike, there was simply no way for me to either get my money or communicate about my penury except via the occasional friend slipping across the Swiss border, Vichy-style, to mail a letter. Today, rather than paging through musty official records in a provincial French archive repository, I search for data or query colleagues around the world from my kitchen table. My monthly stipend, still nostalgically referred to as a "paycheck," is by no means a piece of paper that can be held up by a postal service or a labor action; rather, money and transactions move through cyberspace at a cyber pace. Businesses large and small sell products, seek components, and arrange financing wherever in the world markets offer the best price, and following an electronic handshake, payments can move securely and instantaneously. Distance may not actually have died, but it must be having a harder time causing graduate students to go hungry.

Political forces, too, are part of the wave propelling the current integration of the global economy, even when disequilibrium and indeed dysfunction kick-start those forces. Give credit to disequilibrium and dysfunction, for example, for the pattern of liberalizing market reforms that has spread through many economies in the wake of the Cold War. The events of 1989 in Europe—culminating in the dismantling of the Berlin Wall and the fall of the Iron Curtain—sparked the opening of market-driven economies across Eastern Europe, which soon became a workplace for manufacturers looking for more favorable labor costs. When General Electric opened a lightbulb factory in Ozd in northeastern Hungary in 1998, that was a tip-off that the old Communist-driven notion of centralized planning had given way to the more freewheeling ways of capitalism. More than a decade later, GE has continued to upgrade and expand its Hungarian presence. It's no fluke: Capitalism has taken hold in countries where for generations it was anathema.

The fall of the Iron Curtain also meant that products once controlled by central government planners were privatized and thereby unleashed onto the market. Polish vodka is a case in point. Centrally controlled, even rationed throughout the 1980s, its privatization caused an explosion of production and marketing that caught and rode the upward rise of vodka popularity during the first decade of the twenty-first century. There are people of a certain age, it is safe to say, who would never have imagined that the words "premium luxury vodka" and "made in Poland" would ever go together. That's a newly emerging reality right there.

Among the other newly emerging realities are some of the countries on the EM list—nations that are literally brand-new, a direct result of the dissolution of the Soviet Union, which unlinked the Baltic republics and Caucasus countries from 70-plus years of centralized, Moscow-based control. Places like Belarus, Krygyz, and various of the "Stans"—Kazakhstan, Tajikistan—pulled away from the Russian center and began making concerted efforts to deregulate their own business environment and liberalize their market systems, with noticeable results in terms of growth.

In other cases, crisis was the motivating force. One reason that India and so many of the countries of East Asia are such successful emerging markets is that they experienced—and learned a lesson from—the economic crises that skittered around their continent in the 1990s. India had such a close brush with default in 1991 that it literally had to airlift its gold reserves to the International Monetary Fund as collateral for a loan. The Indian government bounced back with a series of liberalizing reforms, reducing state planning and centralized resource allocation, and its newly unshackled economy was on its way.

But of course, China overwhelms every other story in the scope and impact of its move from a planned to a market-driven economy. Whether or not Deng Xiaoping ever really said that "it's glorious to be rich"[4]—I tend to doubt it—the reforms he introduced following his ascension to power in 1978 unleashed a stunning economic surge. Starting with incentives for farmers, continuing through township and village enterprises and special economic zones, China used its traditional ability to mobilize its population in order to transform its economy and grow at an astonishing rate. China's per capita gross domestic product grew, in purchasing power terms, from $250 or 2.2 percent of the world's output in 1980 to more than $7,500 and 13.6 percent of the world's output in 2010. Adult literacy increased from 65 percent of the population in 1982 to 94 percent in 2009. Infant mortality fell from 46.1 in 1980 to 16.6 in 2009. And I'm writing this book on a computer made and distributed by a Chinese company, Lenovo, but it probably would have been made in China even before IBM sold its PC business to Lenovo. Napoleon more or less predicted all this centuries ago when he described China as "a sleeping giant." "Let her sleep," he said, "for when she wakes, she will shake the world." No kidding.

China, India, Eastern Europe, Brazil, Russia, Indonesia: Hundreds of millions of people are participating in the emergence of these new market economies. They are surfacing upward from centuries of a subsistence existence into a condition of increasing economic where-withal. They are exploiting opportunities they have not had before. They are young, and they are productive. How productive? Check not just your shirt label but the label on your laptop, refrigerator, kitchen knives, the dog's leash, half the parts of your car, even—wait for it!—your kid's baseball glove. Probably all of them tell you what has long been evident—that some 62 percent of the manufactured goods that Americans bought during the five years from 2004 through 2009, the last year for which data are available, were made outside the United States.[5]

The people who make that stuff, all those newly economically enfranchised millions rising from poverty in those newly emerging markets, will themselves increasingly gain spending power. And the evidence is clear that they are eager to spend it. When we talk about finding companies that establish a foothold in rapidly growing markets, this is what we mean.

The Opportunity and the Challenges

In the ongoing transition from labor arbitrage to capital-intensive manufacture, worker expectations and demands for added value rise along with economic growth. The sock manufacturing plant that moved out of North Carolina to China moves next from China to Bangladesh, and from there, who knows? Meanwhile, a whole new bunch of Bangladeshis have found a way out of poverty—and, for possibly the first time in their lives, have money to spend on consumer goods.

Just look at Figure 4.2 to see how the BRICs (and Mexico!) surpass the United States, Western Europe, and Japan in the growth of an emerging pool of middle-class consumers. It's only the beginning, and they're not just consuming DVDs, car loans, McDonald's, and running shoes anymore. The wage earners who priced themselves out of the sock-making business in China have presumably moved on to higher-value positions with higher pay, which they are spending on more and fancier consumer goods. Among them is upmarket apparel like that sold by Burberry, whose famous trench coat is perhaps the quintessential

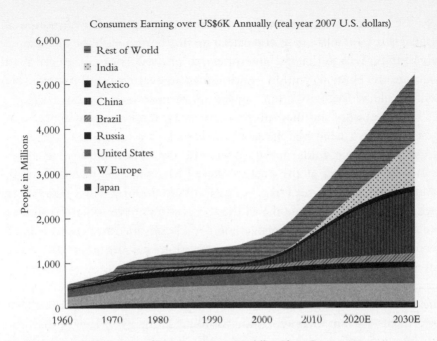

Consumers Earning over US$6K Annually (real year 2007 U.S. dollars)

Figure 4.2 Rapid Growth in Emerging Middle-Class Consumers
SOURCE OF CHART DATA: United Nations, Department of Economic and Social Affairs, Population Division (2011).

symbol of upper-crust British class. The centuries-old clothier, now a global behemoth purveying home décor, gifts, fragrances, and accessories along with the clothing, has almost four times as many retail locations in China as in its native UK, and five times as many in South Korea. No wonder more than 40 percent of total global demand for luxury goods already comes from the emerging markets; that will rise to 50 percent by 2017 and to nearly 60 percent by 2020. If you travel that year, expect to see a lot of Louis Vuitton handbags, Tag Heuer watches, and the aforementioned Burberry trench coats in the heat of New Delhi and Mumbai, as all those Indians turn 30 and buy themselves something special for the occasion. Why not? It's their economic momentum, and they deserve to ride it.

So do China's nearly one million millionaires, a third of them women, whose acquisition of hyper-luxury toys and trinkets is breathlessly reported in the global business press. And so do the fast-growing cities of central Turkey and the impressive entrepreneurs driving the growth, known collectively as the Anatolian Tigers. Ditto for the modernizing regimes of Latin America now realizing economic gains that are putting a certain large northern neighbor to shame. Everything tells us that the emerging markets will continue to claim an ever greater share of world GDP and play an ever more substantive role on the global stage.

So does all of this mean that the emerging markets, growing fast and presumably in need of capital, constitute a good investment opportunity? The simple, initial answer is yes, and the opportunity is big. How can it be measured? In the distance these EM economies have still to go, and in how far they must travel to catch up. How long will it take? Over what scope of development will these economies have to go to produce and sell the goods and services of the classic wealthy, industrialized economies? In the answers to those questions lies the potential of the investment opportunity.

Think of it this way: Only the top 3 percent of the population of India has income greater than the poorest 1 percent of the U.S. population. That represents a game of catch-up that is likely to be even longer than the seemingly endless cricket matches Indians love so much, and it is an enormous investment prospect. So you haven't missed the opportunity to profit from wealth creation in the emerging world. On the contrary: The opportunity has just begun. Remember: The United States became the world's largest economy around 1880 and was still creating some of its greatest investment opportunities more than a century later.

Does that mean you should close this book, call your broker, buy into an India investment fund, and wait for the returns to pour in? Not quite. The simple answer—that EM is the place to invest—is not without its challenges. In the succeeding chapter, as promised, we will look at how to think about investing in EM—that is, what to do when you have decided you're ready actually to put money on the line. But before you can get to that decision, you need to understand the challenges to the ongoing economic growth of these markets. The transformation from poverty to the middle class, from labor arbitrage to capital-intensive manufacture, is rarely a straight upward line. It does not usually happen easily, and it will not happen in the same way everywhere. There will be roadblocks. Some of these economies may well falter, and companies that stake their futures in those economies will falter as well. Investors must therefore be wary of the traps on the path to growth. Here are some of the principal traps that can snare the unwary.

A Bit of Caution

Political stability is an ongoing issue in most rapidly growing countries even if it just simmers beneath the surface. Stick with our India example where conflict is very much in the open: The explosive growth that large segments of the population are enjoying at this moment has also left behind an estimated 600 million people still living in poverty in rural villages—a potential flashpoint of political pressure if a rising tide of inequality spurs resentment. Meanwhile, the Indian version of democracy makes U.S. federal policy making seem almost functional, and while the so-called license raj is supposed to be a thing of the past—the elaborate red-tape network of licenses, permits, and regulations that even a single individual had to navigate just to start a business—a ponderous bureaucracy and its nasty but faithful companion, corruption, nevertheless continue to impede the establishment and expansion of business in India. Whether recent moves in response to major protests to create an independent corruption agency help to address this ongoing weakness in the Indian economy remains to be seen.

Some of the Eastern European economies have not been self-ruled democracies for very long; they're still new at the game, and they could stumble. Regime change can prove unfriendly not just to the losers in the political struggle but to the businesses, foreign and domestic, that prospered under the old regime. Countries with strong authoritarian or one-party rule face different issues. In China, unemployment and inflation, especially the rising cost of food and housing, occasionally burst into protest. Thus far, this "jasmine revolution" has been both politically suppressed and psychologically becalmed by policies aimed at bringing employment, housing, and health care to less developed regions, but trouble hovers under the surface and sometimes finds its way into the newly paved streets.

Inflation is a danger and a worry throughout the ranks of EM stars— Vietnam and Brazil among them—and the trade-off between it and growth is not always easy, politically palatable, or achieved successfully. Just as my fellow Nebraskan William Jennings Bryan and the Wizard of Oz (in the book, Dorothy's magic slippers were silver, not ruby) may have thought that free silver and an end to the gold standard would make money plentiful and save the struggling farmer and factory worker, loose monetary policies can still seem a politically attractive way of maintaining growth in tough economic times. In reality, an accelerating and

unpredictable price spiral disproportionately penalizes the poorest segments of the population, while at the same time it inhibits investment and
growth. How eager would any of us be to risk expanding our businesses
when we couldn't predict what we'd later be paying our workers and
suppliers or how quickly we'd be able to raise our own prices?

Of course, inflation isn't only an emerging-economy issue. In the
United States and Europe, central banks have responded to debt crises
by significantly expanding their balance sheets—printing money, in
plain speech. While the response has been valuable in both cases, once
the crisis period has passed (and it will pass), investors must watch
carefully to see if central bankers will avoid the temptation to allow
today's balance sheet expansion to become tomorrow's free-silver, easy-
money regime. Sopping up the money they've created before it begins
to fuel inflation will be as important to financial stability as were the
money-creation measures they took as the crisis deepened.

For the United States and the Eurozone, that policy crossroads is still
in the future. The growth-inflation trade-off, however, poses a more
immediate policy tightrope for several rapidly growing economies.
Almost everywhere, central bankers responded to the financial crisis and
subsequent recession by cutting interest rates to stimulate the local
economy. With growth resurgent but uneven, policy makers everywhere find it difficult, as a former Fed chairman famously said, to take
away the punchbowl just as the party's getting going. The temptation
will always be there to keep monetary policy too easy too long. Central
bankers walk a tightrope with recession on one side and inflation on the
other. Not all will maintain their balance on that policy tightrope,
especially when the punchbowl has been out too long. Investors will
have to take account of the inflation that could follow.

Red tape at best and corruption at worst also plague a number of the
emerging-market economies, and economic growth can be confounded
by both. Transparency International, the Berlin-based nongovernmental
organization that monitors "the degree to which corruption is perceived
to exist among public officials and politicians," as its website puts it
(www.transparency.org), casts something of a shadow over several of the
burgeoning economies we've been marveling at. In its 2010 corruption
ranking of 178 countries—with Iraq, Afghanistan, Myanmar, and
Somalia at the bottom, and Denmark, New Zealand, and Singapore at
the top—Brazil ranks sixty-ninth, China seventy-eighth, India eighty-
seventh, and Indonesia one hundred and tenth (the United States ranked

twenty-second).[6] It's easy on the one hand to make moral judgments about corruption, or on the other to argue that it's simply an artifact of regulations that don't make economic sense and need to be swept away with the broom of free capitalism. From an investor's point of view, though, corruption drains away profits and potential returns; investing in places where it runs rampant requires special care and discernment.

A case in point is Indonesia, notorious for its rampant business and political corruption—a remnant of its colonial past and especially of the 32-year Suharto dictatorship, during which Indonesia became virtually a family-owned cash machine for the president and his relatives. With one of the oldest oil industries in the world, Indonesia has long been a net exporter of petroleum. As is not uncommon in former colonial economies, the industry is managed on a production-sharing basis: The state-owned entity in charge of the industry, Pertamina, contracts with foreign firms to operate the drilling on government-owned sites in return for a portion of the profits. As is also not uncommon in these situations, Pertamina is something of a patronage mill, doling out the drilling concessions, sales contracts, service contracts, jobs, and influence. The patronage is not just a fact of life; it has become the main support for the structure of the oil industry itself. The result is that Indonesia is now a net importer of oil, while the industry itself is in dire need of investment in new and more efficient production.

There is evidence that Indonesia, still rich in energy resources, is making some headway against this culture of corruption. A Corruption Eradication Commission, established in 2002, has instigated a series of investigations of alleged bribery among the ranks of police and other officials, and certainly a number of business leaders are aware that corruption is a drain on the economy. The story is told of the newly appointed head of Bank Mandiri, who, on arrival in his position, ordered that at least one wall of every office be replaced with glass. The message was clear: Bank Mandiri, at least, would be subjecting managers' actions to the cleansing daylight of open and instant visibility. Bribery was going to be very tough to do, and it would not be tolerated.

In fact, Indonesia's banks tend in general to be professionally managed and are well capitalized, perhaps because, at least since the Asian financial crisis of 1997, private ownership and international participation have been the norm. It has meant that competent, experienced bankers have long been on hand, so as the government continues to divest its ownership in tranches, Indonesian banks have produced excellent returns for investors. That integrity and effectiveness go hand in hand, and that Indonesia's banks evidence this, are rightly points of pride in the Indonesian financial community.

If the lesson of Indonesia seems to be that abundance, in the form of oil, spurs corruption, whereas scarcity—capital, in Indonesia's case— avoids it, the exact opposite is true in China. There, the desperate appetite for oil and the need for efficiency in satisfying that appetite have spawned a couple of well-run, efficiently performing state-owned enterprises. The China National Offshore Oil Corporation (CNOOC) is perhaps the star in terms of both rational and efficient operation and financial performance. Involved in oil exploration, development, and production, the CNOOC performed well over the first decade of the twenty-first century, with an enterprise value rising fivefold from $6 billion in U.S. dollars in 2001 to $99 billion at year-end 2010. Another good performer is China Petroleum, a refiner and petrochemical producer. First, it tripled its enterprise value from 2001 to 2010—from US$48 billion to US$128 billion; second, it did so partly by shrinking the number of its employees from half a million to fewer than 375,000, thereby demonstrating a commitment to efficiency and productivity along with the value growth.

By contrast, banks in China, where capital is abundant, are a black box, the internal workings of which remain a mystery. Bank balance sheets are simply not credible; as I write this, Chinese banks trade at roughly half the valuation of their emerging-market peers. It doesn't compute. And everyone seems to know that lending to political associates, especially those involved in highly leveraged development projects, is profligate. But above all, these are state-owned enterprises operated for purposes of public policy; if the government suddenly needs to bail out the construction boom, for example, that is where the capital will go, making China's banks a dangerous bet by any definition.

Meanwhile, take your pick for how corruption happens: scarcity, abundance, human nature. However it seeps into a nation's economy, it is damaging and dangerous, sapping economic strength even as it undermines human rights and potentially putting the kibosh on investment yields. For investors, therefore, the presence of corruption in an emerging market in which you may be interested in investing rightly raises a big red flag. It is an added risk to the investment—one that is difficult to measure and impossible to manage. Be warned, and be aware.

Lack of appropriate skills can be almost as damaging as corruption. A joke runs through the chic wine bars of the Indian tech city

Bengaluru—Bangalore, to most of us—claiming that a sign outside the walls of one of the city's technology outsourcing campuses reads, "Warning: Trespassers Will Be Hired." It's a sarcastic reference to the shortage of available workers with entry-level technical skills—despite the accomplishments of India's ambitious plans to create scientists and engineers who can propel the country's economic development. The Indian Institutes of Technology rank among the finest engineering schools in the world, and the Institutes' graduates are indeed more than capable of propelling that economic growth, but the growth still needs workers on the line who can master basic technical skills, and the average Indian adult has only 4.4 years of schooling,[7] which is simply not enough. Again, while economic growth and human capital development tend to go hand in hand, mismatches do occur. When they do, the unemployed become restless, and companies grow more slowly than their markets might allow. Investors, beware.

Infrastructure is another potential minefield for investors. I remember my first experience in Beijing's international airport. It was around the turn of the millennium, and I was changing planes there for a flight to Shanghai. The weather was nasty, and flights were delayed. Anxious passengers stood meekly staring at the state-of-the-art electronic departure board overhead, which regularly flashed flight numbers, destinations, and gate assignments. Unfortunately, there seemed to be no relationship between the information being flashed at us and the instructions being given the flight crews of the planes doing the flying. The result was that gate assignments rarely reflected the actual destinations of the planes at those gates. I got to Shanghai, but I'm still not quite sure how.

After another decade of enviable infrastructure investment, I'm certain that the problem I encountered is ancient history, and anyone who has spent an hour lined up on the tarmac at a New York City airport or has tried to make an international connection through the mind-boggling maze that is the Frankfurt International Airport will know that emerging economies don't have a monopoly on infrastructure messes. Still, infrastructure deficits continue to inhibit progress in most of these fast-growing countries. China's fatal high-speed rail accident during the summer of 2011 reminds us that all that glitters on roads and rails will not have a golden safety record. Again, investors must account for this friction and temper their enthusiasm, although, as we'll see, today's traffic mess can be tomorrow's investment opportunity. Finding that opportunity will be our challenge.

The Bottom Line

Economies now emerging from subsistence to industrialization to knowledge-based economies represent an investing opportunity; they are places where economic value is being created.

This process has always existed, but it is proceeding today at a historically unprecedented pace. Technology, global trade, and competitive markets are motivating forces behind this transformation.

With growth comes the demand for a rising standard of living and for enhanced goods and services. Businesses that can succeed in such countries by providing those goods and services are in line for a major profit opportunity. Investors who identify those businesses can prosper with them. That opportunity can be measured as the distance these economies must advance in order to catch up to the developed economies.

Different economies will develop at very different rates and will sustain progress with varying degrees of success. Investors must avoid overly broad generalizations. The ability of many of these economies to sustain growth may be imperiled by such realities as:

- Political instability.
- Inflation.
- Bureaucratic entanglements.
- Corruption.
- Skills gaps.
- Infrastructure deficiencies.

Chapter 5

How to Read Your Shirt Label: The Myth and Reality of Investing in Emerging Markets

Willie Sutton famously said he robbed banks because "that's where the money is." Investing is a more honest line of work than Willie's chosen field; it is also more secure. But if you are investing because you seek to raise your standard of living and continually increase your prosperity, then, following the Sutton logic, you must go where the growth is. That is, you must invest in places, enterprises, and activities in which more and more money is consistently being created and circulated, thereby providing an ever-increasing opportunity for profit.

Where will you find growth? You'll find some, even more than the doomsday crowd seems to believe, here in the United States, but it will be slower and less steady growth than we've come to expect. You will not find growth in most of Western Europe. Nor in Japan. Not, in short, in the major economies of what we refer to as the developed world. We have developed ourselves into the metaphoric seven lean years—likely to be longer—that have followed the Great Moderation's years of plenty.

The lean years for these developed economies mean that they are all deleveraging like mad, trying to whittle down the mountains of public and private debt they took on during the years of plenty. For example, as shown in Figure 5.1, Japan's public debt alone is more than 130 percent of its GDP, and the earthquake and tsunami of 2011 will make it even harder for the Japanese government to reduce that burden. Since most of that debt is in domestic hands, the picture dims further as its aging population retires and begins to cash in its savings. Since early 2010, we've all gotten acquainted with debt problems in Europe, but the numbers are worth remembering. In Italy, for example, sovereign debt stands at 115 percent of GDP. In Spain, by contrast, public debt is a mere 60 percent or so of GDP, but private debt is a disaster at 189 percent of GDP.[1] Like

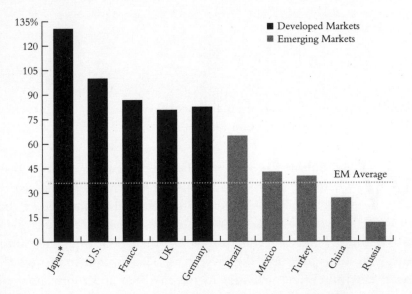

Figure 5.1 Forecasted 2011 Gross Debt as a Percentage of GDP

*Net debt is used for Japan.

SOURCE OF CHART DATA: International Monetary Fund, *World Economic Outlook*. Projections as of September 30, 2011.

Spain, we in the United States are doubly burdened: household and business debt is high, and so is public-sector government debt.

For all these overleveraged economies, the process of unwinding the debt is likely to be secular rather than cyclical—that is, long-term and persistent, not just a phase that passes with the turning of the usual business cycle. And since the deleveragers represent perhaps 60 percent of the world's economy, the economic drag is also likely to be secular, and it is equally likely to be wide-ranging, reaching even as far as the emerging-market economies.

But although the wave of that economic drag is lapping onto the shores of emerging markets, it does not seem to be swamping those economies. Not only are the EM economies pretty much free of the debt overhang weighing down the developed economies, but they are also still growing. That makes the emerging economies the place to find the rapid growth that creates opportunity—both for the long-impoverished populations of those countries and, as we noted in Chapter 4, for investors, wherever they may be, who provide the capital that enables enterprises in those economies to flourish.

But where Chapter 4 described how and why the emerging markets constitute an opportunity for investors, this chapter tells you how to go about seizing that opportunity. For the advice to invest in emerging markets is hardly a novel or an original thought. In fact, "Invest in Emerging Markets!" has been a hot headline for some time. The problem is that too often the story following the hot headline is hot air, filled with exaggeration at best, obfuscation at worst. So in this chapter, I demolish some of the myths surrounding emerging-market investing and illuminate the realities. EM investing is no cakewalk, but executed with a clear eye and a steady hand, it can be a tremendously rewarding answer to fruitlessly following investment habits whose time has passed.

In fact, I argue in these pages that today's emerging-market economies are collectively in a position to experience the very same kind of rising prosperity we in the developed world enjoyed during the Great Moderation. It means that investors who can steer clear of the myths and confront the realities of EM investing can therefore look forward to the same kinds of returns they realized in the investing heyday of 30 years ago.

But there are important caveats to keep in mind if you are to find those returns.

Caveat Emptor

For one thing, there is a slip of logic that tends to slip up investors. Accelerating economic growth in a country has the potential to create income, wealth, and profits. That is unarguable. It doesn't follow, however, that accelerating economic growth necessarily leads to great stock market performance in the country where that growth occurs. In fact, the correlation between a country's per-capita GDP growth and the returns investors realize in its stock market tend to be low, even negative.[2]

To understand the reason for this, follow the money; it may very well flow right out of the emerging-market country. Think about it: Economic growth occurs as new technologies are introduced, new workers enter the formal labor force, and existing workers produce more each hour they work. But the existing companies in the countries where all these changes are taking place may or may not be the ones to profit, especially when the changes occur rapidly. The new wealth may flow to new companies or to foreigners who have already seen comparable changes elsewhere and understand how to profit from them. When you buy a share of stock, always remember that you're buying a piece of a company, not a piece of geography. So when we say it's time to invest in emerging-market economies, the idea is to appreciate the growth and find where the profit from it is being realized, always keeping in mind that profits often accrue far from places where the growth occurs. A Nigerian household's newly earned wherewithal to buy a package of laundry detergent may result in revenues earned in far-off Rotterdam or Cincinnati and may even weaken a domestic competitor that lacks the credibility of an international brand.

Another reality to keep in mind is that for the individual retail investor, investing in emerging markets adds a risk that is qualitatively different from what you're accustomed to. Think of it as the risk of what gets lost in translation, and take it as a rule of thumb that if there is something that *can* get lost in translation, it will. After all, you are dealing with countries representing profoundly different cultures and languages from your own and profoundly different ways of doing business. Moreover, it is presumably out of the question for the individual investor to put in the serious study and to undertake the costly travel that could close the translation gap, just as it is impractical for the individual investor to cultivate the local connections with professionals on the ground in far-off places or to devote 24/7 attention to the markets and to any and all political, social, and economic forces that may affect your investments. That's a full-time job. Several full-time jobs.

There are, however, professionals who do the job full-time, who are equipped with all the resources it takes to do the job, and who have experience in the markets in which you choose to invest. They are there precisely to do the heavy lifting of research and monitoring, and partnering with them can certainly mitigate the translation-loss risk substantially.

Okay, once again I'm guilty of taking a stand that reflects where I sit professionally. But leaving it to the professionals should not mean blithely picking a fund and going home to bed. Due diligence before choosing a fund and due vigilance once the choice is made are essential. That means, at a minimum, devoted reading of the international business press and international business journals, as well as finding a way to stay abreast of developments in that part of the world in which you've chosen to invest. The aim is not only to keep an eye on the investments you've made, but also to keep an eye out for the next emerging-market opportunity. In the Further Reading section at the back of this book, I've noted a few sources of investment information and debate that can be helpful in keeping yourself informed.

Defining the Opportunity

We can measure the investment opportunity in emerging markets, as we suggested back in Chapter 4, by the distance these economies have to go to catch up—to bring substantial portions of their populations out of poverty and into the middle class, to make the transition first from subsistence agriculture to low-wage manufacturing, then from low to higher value-added manufacturing and services, and eventually to innovation and world-class businesses. That process will produce enormous wealth not just for its direct beneficiaries, but also for businesses around the world that facilitate it.

Not all countries we can now call emerging will in fact actually emerge precisely in this way. Indeed, if history is any guide, many won't. But whatever the specific steps a country takes to rise from one level to the next, each step in the process creates opportunity not just for the immediate participants but for the businesses that supply the wherewithal to make these transitions occur. The task for the investor is to find the transitions, assess how far they can go, and then ask who benefits from the economic value they create.

Take as an example electric power in India. In fact, consider just a single aspect of electric power in India—refrigeration, and the impact that extending the reach of refrigeration can have. Stretching the power grid to millions of small marketplaces can vastly increase the available supply of perishable food, much of which now spoils before it can reach the consumer, and can thereby reduce inflation in food prices. It's hard to argue with the social benefit of that, but both the social and economic impact are augmented even further as you then think about who will supply the generating equipment, the transmission lines, and the small refrigerators. Think about the employment all that work could create and the goods and services those workers will purchase. I've only scratched the surface, but I think the point is clear. Advancing economies create opportunity.

So start by measuring how and how fast these economies are advancing. How do you do this? One obvious answer is to look at GDP—both at where the particular market stands in the rankings and at the rate of growth of its GDP—and how much, how fast, and how steadily the economy is expanding from one quarter to the next.

Supply and demand also provide an answer. How much can a particular economy produce, and how much must it buy to do the catching up? Think of the question in terms of the building blocks of economic infrastructure: construction, transportation, power generation, and the like. For example, how much cement does a country produce, and how much must it import to construct the manufacturing plants, housing, and other facilities that qualify the country as in transition to a capital-intensive manufacturing economy? How many power generators—to operate the plants and light the houses—does the country's economy produce, how many must it import, and how fast is it getting them produced or imported? You can track these signs of progress by going to some of the websites I've used to develop the charts and graphs you've been seeing. Start following the progress of countries that appear to be growing, and ask how fast and in what sectors.

It is not coincidental, for example, that in the twenty-first century, China has produced more than half the world's supply of cement, with India a very, very distant second. Nor is it surprising that China is the world's largest consumer of cement, as it continues, albeit somewhat more slowly than in the past, its vast program of construction.

The equally unsurprising but particularly instructive part of the story is that China's cement-producing prowess is being undermined by other emerging-market economies—Thailand, for one—that are selling the product more cheaply. This is the rising-value domino effect of market emergence, and it is and ought to be an essential focus of investing in EM economies. It serves as a barometer of where on the scale of emergence a market is—and of where to look for fresh investment opportunities.

This rotation of low-skill, labor-intensive production from one region to the next also underscores the importance of understanding the specific economics of an investment you're considering. Some commentators, for example, have cautioned against investments in emerging-market companies, citing rising labor costs as a drag on future profits. Maybe, but maybe not. Companies that have developed expertise in finding cheap labor markets may be able to relocate production from their home countries to new low-wage frontiers as these costs shift. Companies headquartered in mature markets have done so successfully; why can't their emerging-market competitors do the same? Effective outsourcers speak many different languages. Always remember you're investing in companies and their competitive advantages, not in countries where they may be headquartered.

Similarly, the opportunities to reach expanding markets aren't limited to the borders of emerging economies, either, nor are those opportunities limited to the raw material and mass production industries we've typically associated with emerging economies. One important example may be in the emergence of a market for health care products and services that the developing world can supply. Despite considerable regulatory obstacles, the demand for cheaper drugs and the ease of obtaining same via the Internet make generic drug production a growth industry. When the cholesterol-controlling prescription drug Lipitor went generic in late 2011, its sales as a brand name plummeted, threatening the economics of its developer, Pfizer, as Lipitor, then the world's best-selling drug, had represented more than a fifth of Pfizer's annual sales. The end of the patent also set off a near explosion of production among companies that manufacture drugs in generic form—postpatent—and most generics by far are produced in the developing world. For investors, there's an object lesson in both Pfizer's loss and the gain by the generic manufacturers. There is also something worth thinking about in the image of all those aging baby boomers sitting in front of their laptops trolling for the cheapest generics they can find, wherever they come from.

Nor are drugs the only opportunity. Patients from the developed world are now traveling abroad to find cheaper medical care than they can get at home, especially for elective surgery. Enough U.S. patients are heading to India or Singapore, Malta or Montenegro to qualify as a trend. They go abroad for plastic, orthopedic, dental, or other surgeries, typically performed by U.S.-trained doctors in technologically advanced hospitals. Even including the round-trip airfare, it still costs these American patients less than the surgery on native ground. This practice even has a name—medical tourism—and has already sprouted a mini-industry. And where there's a growing industry, there are investment opportunities.

Another signal about the character of an EM investment opportunity is some indication of consumer goods consumption—basic goods like clothes, shoes, radios, and the like, of course, but also luxury goods like haute couture, fancy shoes, and flat-screen televisions. We saw in Chapter 2 how quickly and how dramatically a pool of middle-class consumers is forming in a number of the emerging markets—specifically, the BRICs and Mexico. What is equally dramatic is the extent to which consumers in the emerging markets have moved beyond basic consumer goods to luxury goods, reveling in designer clothing, upmarket luggage, watches, jewelry, perfumes, cosmetics, even yachts. The consumption of these goods shows a rising tide of wealth in general and may point to specific industries and even companies that are the beneficiaries of the consumption.

Consumption, of course, requires consumers. In fact, it requires consumers with the wherewithal to buy more than what mere survival demands. Getting to that point in turn requires a population with the health and skills to produce goods and services that someone else wants to pay for. Consequently, measures like literacy rates, longevity, and nutritional adequacy, which concern us from a humanitarian point of view, also matter from an investment perspective as we search the world for economic progress. India, for all its progress, will still find its growth limited as long as the majority of its females over the age of 15 cannot read and write. A world away in Guatemala, more than one child in six under the age of five shows symptoms of malnutrition,[3] and until that changes, Guatemala, too, must face decades of limited opportunity.

These caveats are reminders to investors to step carefully. They also make it all the more important to know what to look for when exploring these emerging markets for investment opportunities.

What to Look For

Investing is about looking for an edge. That's what investors do: They try to identify a company they think has created a distinctive advantage in technology, or branding, or market access, or productivity—any or all of the key signals of a moneymaking idea we talked about in Chapter 3.

Transitions, like those that define emerging-market economies, are full of edges, but they don't often look like those traditional signals of competitive superiority. They look instead like disjunctions, discrepancies from an established norm, even anomalies. I earlier compared the redistribution of the centers of economic growth in the world to the large-scale motions of geologic activity, and the metaphor is particularly apt for the kind of disjunctions occurring in emerging-market economies. In geology, shifting tectonic plates constantly slide into, over, and under one another, and as they do, changes occur at the boundaries of the plates. In the advance from subsistence to middle class, from labor arbitrage to capital-intensive manufacture, constantly shifting economic forces bump up against the old, established cohesion of poverty. In those moments when the shifts break down the established cohesion, investment opportunities tend to show up on the boundaries of the breakdown.

So start by seeking out incongruity. Find the lag in infrastructure investment—the soft underbelly of China's rush to construct airports with every modern convenience, except—the lag—that the information board gives out wrong information. Or worse: the infrastructure deficit that led to China's disastrous rail accident in 2011.

As countries like China deal with mishaps and disasters by reorienting public investment from an emphasis on speed and size to an emphasis on quality, opportunities for investors emerge.[4] Look for businesses that have learned to cope with these infrastructure lags, to make a virtue of necessity. For example, why does India do a much better job of exporting services than of exporting goods? If you've ever driven anywhere in India, you know the answer. Electrons carrying information from call centers, medical laboratories, or software developers can move around the world at speeds approaching the speed of light. Indian trucks, goods carriers, can often move only at the speed of the oxcart on the road in front of them. If you were an entrepreneur, where would you risk your time and capital? Look for similar discrepancies or incongruities in other areas of transportation, housing, power generation, port facilities, mining—all the engines of infrastructure that a developing economy runs on.

Another kind of incongruity is the unfair advantage. Many of the emerging-market economies—certainly a number of those now emerging fast in Latin America and Eastern Europe—were the beneficiaries, or in any event the recipients, of a particular kind of policy advice urged on them by the technocrats of developed economies. The advice, characterized by economist John Williamson in 1990 as "the Washington Consensus," meaning that it was imposed by the international financial institutions based in Washington, D.C., fostered reforms that diminished state control and regulation and encouraged economic privatization. But when the privatization happened, a number of companies that had enjoyed centralized government subsidy were left in awfully strong positions, artificially supported by all that public money, to weather the potential storms of a newly deregulated market.

One striking example of that phenomenon is Brazil's Embraer, the military aircraft concern subsidized and then wholly owned by the Brazilian government as far back as the 1940s. Over the years, abundant subsidies and numerous government contracts enabled the company to extend its product line into lighter aircraft and to branch out as a regional airliner. Then, in the rash of privatizing of state-controlled businesses in Brazil in the 1990s, Embraer was sold to private investors, and in 2000, its stock was offered on both the São Paulo and New York stock exchanges. Clearly, the years of subsidy and the ongoing involvement of the government gave Embraer an unfair advantage in expanding its product line and its reach, a definite leg up that has enabled it to become one of the largest commercial aircraft companies in the world. That's the kind of unfair advantage to look for.

In another but significantly different case, the success of the Indian firm Infosys exemplifies what we might call the pretty fair unfair advantage. The company owes much of its success as a global information technology giant to the creativity of its founders. They followed the path we just described and recognized that melding highly trained and modestly paid software engineers with the emergence of speed-of-light global data transmission could create an industry in a country plagued by a huge transportation infrastructure deficit. This brilliant management vision was given a decided boost, however, by the protectionist policies of Indian governments in the 1980s, which gave the fledgling company room to grow. While all the protection a government can muster can't make an inefficient, low-quality producer into a world-beater, it can give an investable unfair advantage to great entrepreneurship. Early protection meant that Infosys was ready to take on the world when Indian governments in the 1990s began to open the economy to global competition.[5]

A word of caution: When the unfair advantage depends on a cozy relationship with an incumbent regime, it can disappear with the speed of a coup, an election, or a heart attack. Unfair advantages can also result in hubris—overreaching the benefits of said advantage and wasting investors' resources on trophy projects. The investment key, as always, is understanding the economics of the enterprise and watching for what might change its profit-making logic.

In fact, as protectionism, statism, and crony capitalism fade, the process of institutional reform of an economy affords numerous moments of investment opportunity—disjunctions at the boundaries. For example, India's planned economy, from its midnight birth in 1947 to its opening up in the 1990s, spawned the license raj mentioned in Chapter 4—the labyrinthine, often bribery-studded bureaucratic morass you had to work your way through if you wanted to start a business, say, serving as a tiffin wallah delivering hot lunches to office workers. The moment that network of red tape was sliced down to a single, simple license that a would-be tiffin wallah could obtain in a day or a week rather than in months of (sometimes corrupt) bureaucratic machinations, it meant more wealth for the tiffin wallah and therefore more wealth being injected into the economy.

Find that moment—that disjunction in the institutional reform process leading to greater efficiency and quicker wealth creation—and you may be onto an enterprise worth investing in. In fact, even better than finding the enterprise benefiting from the first moment of disjunction, find the enterprise building on the success of the first moment of disjunction. Second-best will have wealth-producing efficiencies already built into its business model.

Similarly, the moment when an informal economic sector is formalized, or when even a part of a business becomes formalized, wealth is created—and an investment opportunity is born. When the lone tiffin wallah has become an employee of Cinnamon Foods, delivering veg and nonveg businesspeople's lunches throughout central and south Bangalore, and when Cinnamon Foods has become a listing on IndiaTiffins.com (www.indiatiffins.com), accessible from any computer in computer-heavy Bangalore—in fact, from any computer anywhere in the world—that is a quantum leap in formalization that warrants an investor's interest.

Such formalization of the informal is particularly evident in the retail sector of an emerging-market economy. As the subsistence economy moves to a cash-crop economy, and street markets are replaced by—and swallowed up in—stores, then bigger stores, then supermarkets, retail operations are formalized and productivity advances from a low level to an increasingly high level. For all involved in the process, that creates wealth, and it thus presents an investment opportunity.

Of course, formalization isn't a linear process, especially when it threatens the usually numerous informal businesses that are likely to suffer from its realization. India's recent quick reversal of a decision to allow multibrand retailing (read Carrefour or Walmart) reflects the power of small, traditional businesses. Investors should be alert for opportunities when change occurs but should be cautious about assuming that it inevitably will. Witness the persistence of small-scale retail in Japan, another example of the power of small, locally entrenched businesses in the face of large-scale competitors.[6]

Finally, look for an enterprise's ability to absorb and use technology in innovative ways. Of course, that is something to watch for wherever you invest, but it is a particularly good signal of opportunity in the emerging-market world. Information technology outsourcing by companies in developed economies started out in the 1990s as a cost-cutting afterthought. But all those companies that were planted in Bangalore—Infosys, MphasiS, Cognizant, and the rest—turned it into a way of life. It's unlikely that Western companies that outsource their service centers to Bangalore will ever go back to doing things the way they used to.

Have you heard of Ali Baba? Not the thorn in the side of the 40 thieves but Alibaba.com (www.alibaba.com), the e-commerce platform for small businesses—small so far, anyway. Started in 1999 by Jack Ma, a onetime English teacher from Hangzhou, China, and 17 others as an exchange site where small manufacturers could display and sell their wares, its initial public offering (IPO) on the Hong Kong Stock Exchange in 2007 for US$1.7 billion constituted the biggest Internet IPO since Google went public on the NASDAQ in 2004. As I write this, Alibaba is reported to be "very interested" in buying out its American onetime big brother, Yahoo!.[7]

Whatever the outcome for Alibaba and for Yahoo!, and whatever landmines their investors may have faced, what is certain is that in the emerging markets right now, in the equivalent of a Silicon Valley garage, or in a college dorm room, or in somebody's fertile brain, the next Infosys or the next Alibaba—or maybe the next Apple or Google or Facebook—is being stitched together and readied for the capital markets.

Emerging-Market Debt Investing

Investing isn't only about equities, yet the headlines that trumpet investment in emerging-market stock funds consider investment in emerging-market debt an afterthought, if they mention it at all. In my view, however, there is an opportunity to earn income—potentially more than from stocks—through the real interest rates on bonds issued by the governments of emerging-market countries. Where once investing in emerging-market debt was an exotic enterprise, the policy and market challenges abroad today in more familiar regions—challenges such as so-called financial repression, very low interest rates, escalating sovereign debt burdens, and the like—give investors several reasons to reconsider this once-offbeat idea.

To see why, take a look at your shirt collar. Mine, at least when it has a tie wrapped around it, probably says, "Made in Malaysia," as that Southeast Asian country has developed an industry making high-quality men's dress shirts. This is a classic labor arbitrage example; the labor required for the fine workmanship that makes high-quality dress shirts is cheaper in Malaysia than in the United States. But there is a twist to the story with implications for investors. After I pay for my shirt in dollars, the retailer or the retailer's supplier has to convert my dollars to Malaysian currency, the ringgit, to pay the manufacturer. So when I replenish my wardrobe, I'm not just buying shirts, I'm engaging in foreign currency trading, whether I know it or not.

If, as I expect, the U.S. dollar will tend to lose exchange value over time relative to the currencies of stronger emerging markets such as

Malaysia (currencies of faster-growing countries tend to appreciate relative to the currencies of slower-growing ones), then the dollars I spend will translate into fewer and fewer ringgit to pay the manufacturer. Though the manufacturer may absorb some of that revenue loss, it's likely that, over time, my shirts will become more and more expensive in dollar terms—even if they stay fairly inexpensive valued in ringgit. And you thought you only had to worry about what collar style suited your face.

That connection between currency markets and the goods we buy raises an interesting question: Shouldn't some of my investment income be in the currency I'm ultimately using to buy my shirts? Couldn't I offset the currency exchange risk by buying some ringgit-denominated bonds? Yes, and at the same time I might also pick up some income advantage over the chronically low interest rates I'm finding with U.S. Treasury bonds. That's worth taking some time to consider.

Risk has always been the bugaboo about owning foreign debt. Investors have quite simply been scared to death to buy bonds issued by some small, politically unstable banana republic ruled by a kleptocracy of exploiters. Fair enough, and Malaysia may once have qualified as a classically exploited colony. But as is the case with so many of the economies now coming into their own in the world, that was long ago. For more than half a century now, Malaysia's government has managed the structure of the economy soundly and smoothly, even maintaining relative overall economic stability through the Asian financial crises of the 1970s and the 1990s.

That greater stability is no accident, and it's not limited to a few countries in Asia. Stricter monetary policies are the basis of that financial stability, and such policies are in effect in many countries we once disdained that are now emerging with strong and stable growth. Brazil is perhaps the poster child for the focus on price stability, which has been largely responsible for turning that country into one of the world's fastest-growing economies. Decades of recurring currency and debt crises mixed with bouts of runaway inflation and culminating in the 2001 default by its huge southern neighbor, Argentina, appear to have taught the Brazilians and many of their neighbors an unforgettable lesson; consequently, a sound money policy has become the nation's mantra and its magic bullet. A propos, I like to remind U.S. investors, who have a tendency to direct disparaging remarks at our immediate neighbor to the south, that according to World Bank statistics, Mexico's gross government debt per capita is about one-half that of the United States.[8] It's time to accept that the economic world is changing, and we have to change with it. That means eighty-sixing all those tired old clichés.

It is also true, however, as Harry Truman pointed out, that we economists usually have two hands, and the other hand for those investing in emerging-market debt is the need to guard against inevitable policy mistakes. Arthur Burns, who as chairman of the U.S. Federal Reserve presided over the great inflation of the 1970s, gave a speech after leaving office (ironically in still-Communist Belgrade) called "The Anguish of Central Banking."[9] In that speech, Burns described how the pressure to avoid the pain of an economic downturn can lead central bankers to keep money and credit too easy too long and unleash the

When Vietnam's stock exchange, the very symbol of its successful capitalism, takes the name of its Marxist revolutionary leader, Ho Chi Minh, it's time to accept that the economic world is changing.
Photo by Rachel Webman.

demon of inflation. Tomorrow's perfect hindsight will tell us whether easing monetary policy in the second half of 2011 in countries such as Brazil and Turkey was a prudent response to a weakening global economy or a foolhardy invitation to renewed inflation, but bond and currency markets certainly expressed their fear of the latter. Favorable trends are never sure things, especially when policy makers' short-term interests are at stake.

So we can't pretend that there are no worries at all about investing in emerging markets—either debt or equities. There are.

Caution: Navigating the Minefield

Chapter 4 described some of the broad challenges in the economics of the emerging markets. How do those challenges translate into bombs that can explode in an investor's face? For a lot can go wrong when you invest in emerging markets. Just as the investment opportunities have a different edge to them, so do the investment risks. Sometimes, these risks are rooted in differences in cultural heritage and values; they constitute risks of understanding as much as anything else. Whatever their origin or derivation, they must be taken into account, so if you're putting money on the line for an investment in one of these countries, pay special attention to the following.

To begin with, U.S. and other Western investors cannot count on the kind of accounting and financial reporting to which they have become accustomed. The accounting firm Ernst & Young surveyed chief financial officers worldwide and found "poor disclosure of material information" to be the most commonly cited problem in valuing an investment in "rapid-growth" countries.[10]

So the would-be investor needs to be aware that financial disclosure statements from emerging-market countries may not read the way you typically understand them to read. Or they may read the same way but mean something different. The past few years have given us reason enough for skepticism about financial reporting in countries like the United States, where legislation, regulation, and litigation have decades of history behind them. The skepticism was certainly sharpened by the apparent misstatements from Western governments themselves—prominent among them the government of Greece, birthplace of democracy and open government. But where independent audits may be a novelty, investors need to be especially wary and look to verify whatever they may find in financial reports. Similarly, respect for contracts and for minority shareholders' rights is likely to be less rigorous in many of the emerging-market countries. Again, read the fine print.

Foreign investors need to be particularly cautious as minority shareholders when the majority owner happens to be the government; these are the so-called state-owned enterprises (SOEs). The comment I heard a while back that investing in a Chinese SOE, such as one of the large banks, is comparable to investing in the U.S. Postal Service is at best an exaggeration, but it captures a bit of reality—SOEs will at times behave more like instruments of public policy than like profit-maximizing businesses. Responding to the 2007–2009 financial crisis, for example, the Chinese government instructed its majority-owned banks to significantly expand their domestic lending. A year later, fearing both growing portfolios of questionable loans and an overheating economy, policy makers instructed the banks to reverse course.[11] That's not the kind of partner you want when you're investing for your personal prosperity. Because many of these SOEs have very large market capitalization—lots of shares outstanding times their price—they tend to make up a significant portion of market-weighted equity indexes. As we saw in Chapter 3, investors may not be getting a bargain when they let such indexes "passively" determine their allocation to these state-owned behemoths.

Bottom line: Whether we're talking about the bailout via temporary public ownership of U.S. auto companies or the long-term Chinese government stake in the country's largest banks, private investors must remember that their partner—a government—is investing to achieve public policy goals, not primarily to maximize shareholder returns. When the two kinds of objectives—the public interest and the growth of wealth—line up together, they may lead to the same result in practice, and investors may profit; when they don't line up together, investors may very well lose their shirts. Look out.

In addition to these issues of sovereign governance, corporate governance is also a matter of concern and should be assessed very carefully indeed. As the Enrons and Parmalats of the United States and Europe illustrate, questionable corporate reporting and business practices can appear anywhere, but where shareholders' rights and impartial judiciaries are novel ideas, the risks are even greater. During the writing of this book, I attended an international conference at which Russian president Dmitry

Medvedev spoke of his country's need to improve and regularize the enforcement of legal contracts. If a head of state willingly makes such a statement, investors need to take special care.

Another mine to avoid is that emerging economies tend to be thinly traded markets. In case you were going to invest in one of my shirt-makers, for example, please keep in mind that the New York Stock Exchange trades more value in an average day than the Bursa Malaysia trades in a month. So even if you believe in the efficient-market hypothesis, there are not many buyers and sellers to set the price of an investment and provide the information investors need. The result is that shares may be significantly mispriced at any given moment. That situation can give you an advantage if you happen to be the one with the superior information, but it can put you at a significant disadvantage if you are the other guy. In addition, thinly traded markets tend to be much easier to get into than out of, leaving you vulnerable should you decide to sell.

One more phenomenon to be aware of is the potential fading of the labor-arbitrage advantage the emerging markets now enjoy. As wages increase in those economies—and decrease in inflation-adjusted, real terms here in the United States and in other developed economies—the gains of outsourcing from developed to developing economies begin to pale. Over time, that could shift manufacturing jobs back to the developed world. There is a company in the U.S. southern state of Georgia that produces disposable wooden chopsticks for sale in China. Business is booming. At risk of repeating an important point too many times, keep in mind that the critical issue for equity investors isn't where the work gets done but who profits from it.

We've seen disasters of EM investing in the past, and they should echo a bit in every investor's brain. The direct expropriation of industries by government, as in Venezuela under Hugo Chavez, or the backdoor expropriation of Russian energy companies via denying extraction permits to foreign-owned companies, remains a risk for investors.

Sometimes, privatization goes bad. In Indonesia in 2000, the giant Asia Pulp & Paper (APP), one of the world's largest emerging-market corporate debtors, with massive operations in both Indonesia and China, went bust, losing 96 percent of its value over a 12-month period. The company had used its unfair advantage of government licenses and subsidies not to benefit investors but to spend wildly on acquisitions, especially for its aggressive expansion into China in the late 1990s, as it sought to meet that nation's seemingly insatiable demand for wood products (like disposable chopsticks). Crony capitalism played its part as well, and APP kept on borrowing heavily at high interest rates, issuing billions in debt that it struggled to repay at maturity. The company was simply overextended, and it collapsed. Offshore investors in the holding company were left holding the bag of liabilities, while the operating units held the assets—an instance of the corporate governance/minority shareholder risk mentioned earlier. Even the eventual government bailout wasn't much help.[12]

Then there is the risk that investing in emerging markets may itself become a bubble that in due course will burst, as bubbles always do. With little in the way of attractive investments available in traditional asset classes, investors everywhere have begun looking to emerging-market funds as the only way to go; 2010 saw a real spike in these funds, which were for a time the hottest investment ticket in town. Those jets have since cooled, perhaps as investors in these funds take note of the risk of overindulging and sober up, but it's worth watching out for another rush into emerging-market investing—at least, the kind of rush that can turn into a bubble. Investors must always remember that there is no idea so brilliant that it's worth overpaying for.

The New Great Moderation?

I haven't discussed inflation as a risk, although it is perhaps the one most talked about. For good reason. Rising labor costs and rising prices are occurring throughout the emerging-market world, and the inflation is to be feared for two reasons. First, it saps the wealth that is the object of your investing; second, the social implications of the inflation can be profoundly disruptive.

Global food prices, for example, began to rise sharply in 2010, and ongoing price rises can have serious consequences. Although we are fortunate in our part of the world to have seemingly put famine behind us, it is worth remembering that several countries on the EM list— Bangladesh, Vietnam, and of course China—suffered food crises or serious famines within the lifetimes of today's older population. In China in particular, which, despite its vastness, is able to cultivate less than 15 percent of its land to feed its 1.3 billion people, rising food prices may be just the thing to turn the jasmine revolution into serious protest and—who knows?—even into organized resistance.

For now, however, the impact of inflation in the emerging markets—both social and financial—has been muted. The reason, in my
view, is that the governments of the EM countries have met the inflation
with appropriate policy responses. Burned, perhaps, by the financial
crises that afflicted Asia and Latin America in the 1990s, these governments have positioned themselves to manage countercyclical monetary
policy. In fact, they've gotten very good at it. They know how to apply
an ice pack to an overheating economy and how to warm up one that's
cooling.

The questions need to be asked: Are the economic policy makers of
the emerging markets a new collective Alan Greenspan, a multilingual
Maestro of the put, conducting a disparate monetary policy orchestra
with perfect dynamics? And are today's emerging-market economies
the New Great Moderation—geographically diffuse, multicultural, and
not what we're used to, but acting very much like that never-too-hot,
never-too-cold Goldilocks Environment of 1982 to 2007 that was so
perfect for investing successfully?

My answer to both is yes. The Great Moderation has moved south
and east. EM investing is today's golden opportunity, and now is the
time to seize it.

The Bottom Line

Investing in emerging markets, like investing elsewhere, is more dependent on the strengths of a company you invest in than on the location of its headquarters. In considering investing in emerging markets, look in particular to understand who is positioned to profit from the growth, not just where the growth is taking place.

Some local businesses will enjoy special advantages in language, culture, and business practices that it will take outsiders time to overcome. Consider working with professionals in EM investing, but perform thorough due diligence in choosing an asset manager.

Measure the potential EM opportunity by ascertaining the country's GDP, supply-and-demand figures, consumption, and human development progress.

Look for opportunities in incongruities:

- Infrastructure development.
- A built-in (unfair) advantage.
- Institutional reform.
- Formalization of an economic sector.
- Innovative use of technology.

Consider investing in EM debt for access to higher yields and to protect your purchasing power against the rising prices of imported goods and services.

Remain wary of risks lurking in:

- Reporting and disclosure standards.
- Involvement in state-owned enterprises.
- Weak corporate governance.
- Thinly traded markets.
- Potential for adverse regime changes.
- Inflation.

Always remember: Fast growth doesn't necessarily equal rising profitability.

Chapter 6

There Is Still Profit Among the Rich

D on't write off the old-guard economies just yet, and certainly don't write off the great companies that call those economies home.

Seizing the investment opportunities that the emerging markets are creating should not mean ignoring the investment opportunities in wealthy nations. There is plenty of juice left in the somewhat tired, somewhat aging economies of the United States, Japan, and Western Europe. Just consider the late Steve Jobs, who reportedly kept sketching ideas for new devices virtually to the day of his death—including, poignantly, one that could hold an iPad in a hospital bed. Or talk to any of the 20-somethings I see lined up outside the recently opened New York outpost of the Japanese fast-fashion purveyor, Uniqlo, many of whom, by the way, are carrying iPads, iPods, or iPhones that will fit right in, literally and figuratively, with the high-tech, relatively low-priced, casual clothing and accessories they're waiting to buy.

That's two supposedly over-the-hill economies, the United States and Japan, confidently meeting a lot of youthful disposable income.

In fact, the kind of fast growth we see in the emerging markets is no more a guarantee of an investable opportunity than is the slowing growth of the developed world a mark of the absence of opportunity. Fast growth can sometimes fall short of sufficient profit margin, and slow growth can still cook up investment winners. The failure to recognize those truths typically leads to a classic and costly investment mistake— equating fast growth with a solid investment opportunity. Those dots don't necessarily connect, however, and in the leaps of illogic that follow are the hot air that inflates bubbles and the blind spot that misses valuable opportunities.

When large numbers of investors do confuse fast growth and exciting headlines—or bad news and scary headlines—with true investment opportunities, we should be especially alert. As you can see in Figure 6.1, during the first decade of the millennium, a herd mentality looked almost anywhere for growth and led broad indexes of emerging-market equities to soar, while a flight from risk during 2011 produced the reverse. In both cases, market prices of good and bad companies tended to move with the herd. Our job is to find the real economic value that both herds trample.

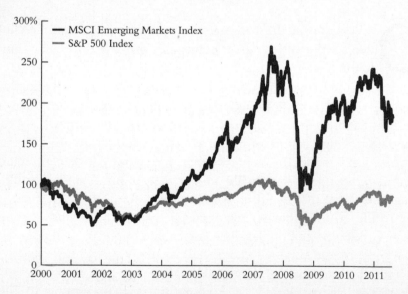

Figure 6.1   MSCI Emerging Markets Index versus S&P 500 Index, 2000–2011
Source of chart data: Haver Analytics, December 31, 2011.

Good Wine in Old Bottles

The truth is that the dull old mature economies convey significant advantages to the entrepreneurs and established businesses based within their borders and legal systems. In this chapter, we remind ourselves of why that's still the case, and we explore what to look for as we search for opportunities.

Let's start with perhaps the most obvious advantage the rich economies bestow on their homegrown companies: size. After all, the United States is still, by a considerable margin, the largest economy on the planet. China is second, and Japan remains the third largest. Germany, France, and the United Kingdom round out the top half dozen,[1] and the European Union as a whole, despite its debt difficulties, constitutes an absolutely huge economy; the EU's 2010 GDP was almost 20 percent larger than that of the United States.

The mere size of the domestic economy can endow a company with a significant head start when it steps out onto the global stage. For example, although many of us think of Japan as a world-beating exporter of cars and consumer electronics, it was the vast domestic Japanese market that gave Toyota, Sony, and their peers the opportunity to develop the scale and invest in the production technology that allowed them to dominate world markets. They cut their teeth on their domestic economy, perfecting their business model at home, and home became the springboard for the global success that followed.

Not that global success *necessarily* follows. When did you last watch a Philco TV? Yet Philco was once a household name in the United States and virtually owned the domestic radio market. It is the company that built the cathedral-shaped "Baby Grand" wooden cabinet radio you still see in movies and TV shows about the 1930s. Iconic it may have been, but it failed just the same. By contrast, did every Chinese family own a Haier wine cellar before these high-end items began to occupy the kitchens of suburban America? Not likely. For this company that started as the Qingdao Refrigerator factory, wine cellars came later; they constituted one of the niches Haier used in its cautious entry into the U.S. market—clearly a phenomenal success. In both cases, however—Philco and Haier—the domestic market provided the base; the investor's job is figuring out who builds scale from that base and who uses it as an excuse for complacency.

More to the point than size, however, is the particular profile of advantages these big, rich economies offer simply because they are rich and highly developed in business and business practices—investment opportunities the fast-growth emerging economies simply do not have. These are advantages that derive precisely from a high level of development, from broad experience and deep expertise in management and marketing, entrepreneurship and service, manufacture and distribution and logistics—skills the emerging economies are still rehearsing. And although we all may at times bristle at burdensome regulation, ponderous legal proceedings, and overly tame corporate boards, in these developed countries, contracts tend to be enforced, regulations tend to annoy evenhandedly, and corporate governance tends to oversee management honestly. Consequently, entrepreneurs and their investors usually get a fair economic shake. The challenge for investors is to identify those enterprises that are using these skills and exploiting these advantages in profitable ways.

Here's a good way to think about it: As we investors adjust our thinking to accept a world of change we can't control, we need to look in the developed world for businesses that are successfully doing the same. Within that vast array of companies with familiar postal addresses, which ones are using the advantages an advanced economy provides—and are thereby adapting to a changed world—and which cannot or will not? We already know we won't find these companies by looking in the same old places and relying on the old shortcuts. Many of the companies we grew accustomed to admiring are simply not in the right arena anymore; I think the previous chapters have established that fact pretty conclusively. Instead, we'll need to look in unaccustomed places for the reframed investment opportunities the developed economies offer—specifically, in three arenas:

First, in the aging populations we've talked about earlier—what they want, what they need, and how both can be delivered to them.

Second, in the provision of high added value—added value at a premium price—deriving from the advanced levels of technological development, potent brand franchise, and entrepreneurship that our old-world economies perfected.

Third, in the new value proposition that began as a down-market, low-price, low- or adequate-quality model and has become increasingly upmarket and higher-quality while maintaining its low price—and in the rising brands that have defined this new proposition.

In each of these arenas, the aim, as always, will be to identify those enterprises that have caught the edge and can deliver the profit advantage. The trick, of course, is in identifying such enterprises early, if possible, but always with an idea to how much you're paying for the opportunity.

Senior Boomers

I've talked repeatedly in earlier chapters about the economic drag an aging population can exert on a mature economy as more workers graduate from the workforce and fewer enter. Now, however, we turn to the market potential inherent in the world's aging population—and therefore the investment opportunity represented by those enterprises that can succeed in that market. It is an opportunity that is only in its infancy, for although the aging demographics are most dramatic in the developed world, the fact is that the median age of the world's growing population is rising everywhere. So is life expectancy. Fifty years ago, in the mid-twentieth century, life expectancy for the populations of the developing world was more than 20 years shorter than that of people in the developed world; today, it is only about 10 years behind—and closing the gap fast. As a consequence, this extraordinary demographic trend will play out over a very long time. Already, however, the outlines of what this means in terms of investment opportunity are becoming clear—in particular among the elderly in the United States, who constitute a well-defined market and a huge target for investment activity.

We're back to *Time*'s Man of the Year, the "pig in the python," that huge demographic bulge that was the postwar shock wave of births around the world, but especially in the Western world. (Japan, too, its population decimated and impoverished after its defeat in World War II, came back strong with its own baby boomers, who turned that nation into a manufacturing powerhouse, and Japan, as we have seen, is today the world's oldest country—a clearly defined, ready market of old people.) In the United States, the baby boomers number more than 78 million people born between 1946 and 1964. The first of them turned 50 in 1996 and will become eligible for full retirement benefits under Social Security in 2012. In much of Western Europe and in Japan, retirement begins even earlier, so as I write this, all over the world (but especially in the wealthy nations) the ranks of pensioners just keep on growing. And businesses everywhere are falling all over themselves trying to figure out how best to serve and profit from these senior boomers. They would be foolish not to.

Virtually from the moment of their emergence, the baby boomers have been studied, analyzed, probed, and profiled. What they wear, what they eat, their lingo, their music, and their politics have been dissected by psychologists, sociologists, economists, marketers, and politicians eager to understand—and cater to—their needs and desires.

That's because the baby boomers are so different from all the generations that came before. Just ask them. They have always claimed a distinctive generational identity—indeed, a generational exceptionalism—and this exceptionalism, they will tell you, has an impact and an influence that go well beyond their sheer numbers.

What really defines them, the baby boomers say—and the varied analysts of their character pretty much concur—is that they constitute the first generation in history to have grown up with television, the birth control pill, the threat of nuclear annihilation, and the promise of the Space Age. Instant information and entertainment at home at the click of a button, sexual freedom, the uncertainty posed by a nuclear sword of Damocles constantly hanging over them, and the ubiquity of technology in every aspect of their lives have shaped the boomers' unique perspective and influenced their attitudes and actions.

This mélange of threat and opportunity makes them open to experimentation, social as well as technical, and to change. It's what keeps them resilient, tolerant, optimistic, and eternally capable of self-improvement. It's why they are skeptical of tradition, why they embrace innovation, and why they insist on directing their own lives. Whatever strikes them as deficient or broken—from their health to the water heater, from career to marriage to outdated software—they're prepared to fix, change, toss, or in some way or another handle all by themselves.

Now that they are becoming the world's elderly, senior boomers still carry those attitudes and perspectives, as ongoing studies of this population cohort make clear. True, they remain, as they have always been, socially divided and politically polarized. But in the eyes of businesspeople—and of those who invest in businesses—they constitute a fairly cohesive market, a bigger elderly market than any generation before them, and, again thanks to rising longevity, a market that will be around for a good long while.

Right now, they control as much as 60 percent of the nation's net wealth and preside over anywhere from 40 percent to 50 percent of all discretionary income, spending in the United States alone somewhere north of $60 billion a year. They are spending it on a disproportionate share of electronic devices, apparel, furnishings and appliances, eating out, eating in, over-the-counter health and beauty aids, and of course medical services and prescription drugs. They're into cruises and other forms of tourist travel, exercise facilities (and cosmetic surgery when the exercise fails), and self-help books and continuing education in one form or another. So, far from going gently into that good night of their golden years, they are arming themselves to fight their way through it, step by step.

Or, as one of my colleagues continually reminds me, people need to hear, see, and chew, and the older they get, the more assistance they need to do those things.

One manufacturer estimates that more than 85 percent of hearing-loss cases result from aging.[2] My wife would be happy to offer me as an example of this phenomenon. At least I think that's what she said. If it is, I might tell her how the old hearing aid has morphed into a slew of high-tech, high-quality "hearing solutions," and how the old hearing-aid industry has evolved into a huge and hugely profitable global undertaking that is growing in all markets, including the emerging markets. Not surprisingly, people in all corners of the world want to hear and will pay to be able to do so, a good basis for ongoing growth. They want hearing devices that are smaller and less visible, and they want not just amplification but compensation for their very specific inabilities to separate sounds or to hear the lower-decibel levels or to capture the high-pitched acoustic guitar riff under the percussion. Call it a case of the generation that perhaps killed its hearing at high-decibel rock concerts wanting to spend its golden years listening to all that golden-age music again.

Whatever the motivation, the technology is continuing to develop to give them these advances, and each subtle technological advance spawns a new product line and a new audience—quite literally—that expands the market even further. In 2009, for example, the successor to the oldest hearing-aid company in the world, founded in 1904 in Denmark by a man whose wife was suffering hearing loss, won the contract to supply the hearing aids to the U.S. Department of Veterans Affairs. The government will distribute these devices to those who have served in our armed forces; that's going to be a lot of hearing aids, and it promises a lot of growth.

Billions more people worldwide need dentures or other forms of dental devices so they can chew—and can thereby defuse an effect of aging that, despite the chortling denture commercials on television, is probably not all that amusing a deficiency to those who suffer it. Dental implants, in fact, may supplant dentures because senior boomers find dentures such an unpleasant throwback. Whatever they use, the boomers want to chew, and demand for help in doing so is growing rapidly around the world.

While chewing, seeing, and hearing may fade with age, vanity demonstrably does not. If you don't believe me, check out the proliferation of those specialized cosmetics stores in the malls; they're not pitched to the young, nor are their products priced for same. Then stroll through the skin-care sections in those shops or the equivalent in your local chain pharmacy. Acne-fighting systems for adolescents have given way to moisturizers and antiaging lotions, creams, gels, or solutions.

And of course, when all of it stops working, the senior boomers need medical tests, medical services, surgery, and replacement body parts. That spells growth for companies that produce the artificial hips and knees and shoulders, or that manufacture the surgical tools and testing equipment.

In short, this is a market that can reasonably be assumed to be interested in products and services that will serve both its fantasies of leisure—helping it satisfy its varied interests in grandchildren, travel, learning, socializing, and the like—and the reality of its diminishing physical and mental powers. So it would surely not be amiss to look for enterprises that successfully provide such products and services.

That is going to take some entrepreneurial creativity. The ongoing studies that continue to probe and profile this generation show that the optimism senior boomers feel about the potential richness of the years ahead is shadowed by disquiet about physical, mental, and financial weakness as the years go on—the downside of the promise of longevity. True, with the can-do resilience they've always shown, worried senior boomers—one in three of them, anyway—say they are fighting the negative effects of aging through physical and mental exercise, nutrition, and other lifestyle changes.[3] The financial debility is another matter, however, and most admit that they have been less than rigorous in planning how to adjust to dwindling resources.

A key 2007 study by researchers at McKinsey & Company found that "only about a quarter of the boomers are financially prepared for their twilight years."[4] These affluent households, with a net worth of more than a million dollars, are well positioned to maintain their current lifestyle in retirement and have every confidence that they can do so. Another quarter of the boomer population consists of those in a totally disadvantaged position for maintaining their current lifestyle who have virtually no confidence that they will do so. That leaves fully half of senior boomers financially unprepared for retirement and split, says McKinsey's report, between those aware of their lack of preparation and those blithely unaware of it.

Sixty percent of boomer consumption, the report concludes, will come from this financially unprepared (and in some cases unaware) majority. This suggests two things to me: first, that a lot of boomers will be looking for work in their retirement, and second, that they are going to be budgeting their finances in ways they have not done before. These are changes that businesses seeking to serve this market had best keep in mind and that investors looking for successful businesses must put on their screening checklist.

Another interesting fact that emerges from the McKinsey study is the number of single-person households in this population. Given the high divorce rate in the United States over the past several decades, this is perhaps not surprising, but McKinsey projects that 46 percent of all boomer households are single—divorced, widowed, or never married. This, too, may be a perspective-shaping circumstance of which businesses should be aware. It is why we are already seeing new concepts of housing and community (e.g., single-story homes in communities where driving a car won't be necessary) and Internet-based affinity groups geared to elderly socializing, health, and travel (Facebook for the senior boomers). Again, social changes of this magnitude create tremendous economic opportunity. If you're wondering where to look for that entrepreneur who has the idea but needs the capital, this is one of the places to start.

It seems evident that in the two main concerns of this growing band of elderly, money and health, altogether new kinds of offerings are going to be needed—comprehensive and comprehensible, capable of being self-directed, and viable over what is expected to be a long term. The businesses that can deliver such offerings first or best are likely to seize the edge in this enormous market, and they are the kinds of companies most likely to reward their investors.

On the money side, my own industry—asset management— confronts a substantial challenge where the senior boomers are concerned, and that challenge is something investors in asset management firms need to keep in mind. The frustrating vice that threatens to pinch the boomers—high expectations and scant financial wherewithal to fund those expectations—challenges us to provide underresourced baby boomers with the financial growth opportunities they want while offering the protection against loss they need. At a minimum, we need to provide a greater degree of predictability about how much purchasing power your accumulated wealth, however scant or ample, can provide—a tall order. As we and our competitors pursue that investment version of the holy grail, there are two implications for everyone else. First, investors need to analyze the investment products that try to achieve this balance very carefully. The best minds in the business won't be able to provide you a free lunch and make a profit doing so. There will be risks in the best solutions we can offer.

Second, some asset managers will be more successful than others in developing suitable investment products for financially challenged senior boomers, and the ones who do so will enjoy some attractive profit opportunities for their owners. The successful asset management companies (that, unlike my own, are open to public investors) may themselves be attractive investment choices for those of us seeking to benefit from an aging trend that we can't change.[5] As you consider the attractiveness of those products, think about who profits from offering them to you.

The Premium-Value-Added Advantage

When I get a little bleary-eyed writing (I hope it's not happening as you read), I can minimize my word processing application, open a web browser, and shop the wares of the world. I can find a virtual community of like-minded shoppers who will tell me where to find the best value. If there's something I want, I can hunt around until I find the best price and the cheapest shipping cost. In this world, a vendor will be hard-pressed to extract a high price, and everyone's profits are squeezed. If profits are thin, investors' returns will probably be disappointing as well. Pricing power, the sustainable ability to collect a premium price from a sufficiently large public, is a rare feature of this new world—rare but not extinct. The search for pricing power brings me to a second arena in which the rich nations hold an advantage that some enterprises may turn into an investable opportunity: what I call premium value added.

Plain old value added is the enhancement that augments a product or service—the momentary advantage that makes a mousetrap a better mousetrap. What I'm talking about is the unassailable advantage that takes the product or service beyond the realm of commodity and endows it with the character and price tag of something at a premium.

What constitutes an unassailable advantage, the kind that warrants a premium price and the premium brand distinction? Some of it is just brand history, for want of a better word. French wine is probably always going to be a top-of-the-line mark of refinement and taste; the wines of other nations may match some French wines, or may even exceed them in quality, but the brand—French wine, Bordeaux, Champagne, France itself—remains unassailable for a range of other associations.

Technological advantage is another key way to achieve premium value added; that is, the product can do something that a commodity simply cannot do, or does it so much better that the superior quality is itself a distinction. You pay a premium for your Apple device not just because it offers superior design and functioning, but because it is always on the leading edge of the technology. Along with the product, you buy the assurance, or at least the perception, that your neighbor won't show up tomorrow with a cooler, higher-functioning version of the same gadget.

Consumers expect that of Apple, for example, and they willingly pay extra for it. Yes, when Mac laptops were first into the market with the built-in camera, they had a better mousetrap: You didn't have to buy a separate webcam and the cable to fit it to your computer and the software to make it work. By itself, that little innovation was a momentary advantage; it lasted the minute and a half it took other laptop manufacturers to catch up. But more than that was involved. What really mattered was another fulfillment of the expectation that Mac would be first and others would have to follow, an expectation that had long been unassailably part of the brand, as built into the Apple brand identity as the camera is into the laptop, the iPod, the iPad, and the iPhone. A brand identity that brings together superior quality and consumer expectations of continuous technological breakthrough constitutes a distinctive level of value added that warrants a premium price. Companies that can do that have pricing power, and their investors have the opportunity to share in the resulting profits.

Companies in the wealthy nations are past masters at producing and marketing such premium value-added products and services. Think of

Lexus, Tiffany, or almost anything Italian you can carry or wear. It is an advantage that cannot be easily or quickly replicated, which means that this is an investment opportunity the emerging markets are not going to be able to offer for a long, long time. It takes years—even generations—to create and maintain the kind of quality such premium products represent and to accrue the brand distinction. (Cult status for the Apple brand probably dates from the release of the Apple II in 1977; the France brand goes back at least to the seventeenth century and Cardinal Richelieu, if not before.)[6] It takes the kind of investment in research and development—and the leisure for creativity—for which emerging economies playing catch-up have neither the time nor the inclination. It takes universities with established laboratories and faculties, a tradition of entrepreneurship, a history of luxury, and the taste for luxury.

I am talking about products that are not simply exceptional per se; in addition, ownership of the product says something about the owner, and this adds to the premium value added. After all, just about any car you can buy anywhere on earth—even the determinedly unpretentious Lada of Soviet Union fame—will get you from here to there. But if you drive a BMW, you paid an enormous premium to do so. You did so because you appreciated owning a machine that works perfectly, with all the power and safety and features you want. But it is also the case that when you are behind the wheel, you are seen as someone who is discerning and successful, or perhaps as someone successful enough to be discerning, the discernment maybe measured in the premium you have paid. Either way, the fact of ownership bestows on you attributes beyond the mere possession of a commodity and bestows on BMW a premium price.

It is unlikely that the consumer's urge to possess both the top-of-the-line item *and* the subtext inherent in possessing it will ever go out of style, so premium value added is an investment opportunity for the long term. Far from decaying, the phenomenon is gaining new force from the growing wealth we've described in the emerging markets. In fact, one of the best ways to profit today from the shift in the world's economic geography is to grab a piece of the expansion of the premium value-added strategy into the most rapidly growing economies. Take a walk along Huaihai Road in Shanghai. You'll see Westerners ducking down side streets in hopes of finding knock-off bargains while the locals browse through the European luxury goods emporiums that line the avenue. If I'm part of the first generation in my family to have disposable income, I want the world to know. What better way to do this than to sport the labels that shout out my prosperity?

Those labels still get attached, however, in the tired old developed countries. Who do you suppose is profiting from the fact that Asia, whose population is genetically more prone to myopia than Westerners and where disposable income is on the rise, is the fastest-growing market on the planet for sunglasses and eyeglasses? Designer frames are now being made that fit Asian facial features, but the designers themselves, the ones who command the premium design fees, still work out of palazzi in Rome or Florence or Milan.

True, premium items sometimes run the risk of becoming commoditized. In the 1980s, rampant overlicensing very nearly brought down Gucci, once the pinnacle of luxury fashion, by debasing the brand to the point that it became the punch line of a joke, expressed in consumer novelty items that ripped off the name with a smirk—and with impunity. Remember the Gucci Gucci Goo infant feeding bibs and the cloth tote bags labeled "Goochy"? The company was eventually brought back from the brink of bankruptcy to very impressive profitability, but the premium value added had been tarnished and weakened; it wasn't easy to redefine it, much less regain it. The example serves as an object lesson on the nature of premium value added; it is the premium you have to watch over.

Nor is it solely products off a shelf that carry premium value added. All the media and intellectual-property industries represent an investment opportunity in which the rich, developed nations have staked out a clear advantage. We in the United States may outsource customer service call centers to India, but India still outsources its creative advertising to Madison Avenue. And in movie-mad India, you can be sure there are more theaters showing American movies than there are theaters in the United States showing Indian movies. Even in the hometown of Bollywood, as I write these lines, one-quarter of the 20 movies showing in more than one theater were from the United States—plus one from the United Kingdom and one from Australia.

The global dominance of American pop culture is routinely deplored, but it remains an unassailable advantage. We produce ideas and innovations. We also, famously, take the ideas and innovations of others and figure out how to sell them everywhere. Movies, musicals, the Internet, and social media all took shape in the United States and have fanned out across the planet. As I write this, at least two key industries, entertainment and publishing, are in the throes of fundamental transformations driven by revolutionary changes in the way their products are delivered. Investment opportunities abound in such industries—along with investment risks.

Affordable Quality, or the Upmarket Mass Market

It is called the "shift to value," and today, it means that consumers are demanding a combination of low price and high quality. That is, of course, a very attractive idea, but the shift to value didn't actually start that way. In the beginning, the shift found consumers looking for lower prices and accepting adequate quality—a trend first noted in the United States in the 1970s, when the Japanese began selling their cars—at cheap prices!—in the United States. Japanese cars in the 1980s were still cheap, but the quality had improved markedly, and by the 1990s, Japanese imports, still lower-priced than American brands, were seen as superior in performance and reliability.

The pattern was followed also in Japanese and later other Asian-manufactured consumer electronics products, and by the turn of the century, the formula had been adopted by the big-box retail stores like Walmart and Target in the United States, and Aldi and Asda in the United Kingdom and Europe. The formula has also made a big splash in the skies—witness Southwest Airlines, JetBlue, and Ryanair; in the computer industry—Dell and Acer; in do-it-yourself stock trading—just check out E★Trade and TD Ameritrade.

In the Great Recession, the shift to value appears to be everywhere. The ever-multiplying number of Spain-based Zara or Sweden-headquartered H&M stores in U.S. cities attests to the pervasive desirability of trendy fashion when it is affordable, while the leapfrogging and much ballyhooed openings of Uniqlo stores in major world capitals manifest how very cool it is for clothing to be not just stylishly trendy but also green and technologically advanced—and still low-priced.

The investment attraction in the shift-to-value formula is that it has the seeds of its own growth within it. As consumers rush to take advantage of low prices, and the value players, supported by high-volume sales, find ways to increase quality at those prices, they create foundations of increased productivity, superior execution, and better practices and procedures that enable them to achieve altogether better economics—to cut costs and enhance quality even further. Traditional competitors, meanwhile, can do little to emulate these value players and are left to compete almost solely on price, which is unsustainable.

This ability to be upmarket to a vast market is a unique advantage of the rich, developed economies. Not unlike premium-value-added providers, value providers have gone beyond the level of commodity, but in their case by identifying competitive advantages within the business model itself—in aspects of execution that change the consumer's experience and thus his or her perception. Take Southwest, for example, which seems to have given considerable thought to what matters to travelers. You cannot reserve a seat ahead of time on a Southwest flight, but you have more choice of departure times, your luggage flies for free, and no-frills flying and arrival at a lower-cost, less crowded airport are both definite advantages to many travelers. And all that is before we get to flight attendants who tell jokes while ordering you to buckle up. Then there's the less quantifiable I'm-beating-the-system aura Southwest somehow conveys, along with its let's-lighten-up stock ticker symbol, LUV. At a time when television shows remind us of air travel's lost luxury (without mentioning today's much more affordable ticket prices), the value-plus-quality branding just works. All of this may be why Southwest increased its market share from 3.2 percent to 14.7 percent between 1990 and 2011, and why it ranked number one in revenue per passenger mile flown as of July 2011.[7] But beware. How far all that advantage over the so-called legacy carriers can extend into the future is a question LUV's executives have begun to ask; it is also a question investors should always ask before risking their funds on a company that depends on cost and perception for its competitive edge.

The shift-to-value formula seems an idea whose time has come—especially in an era in which U.S. and European consumers are eager to lower their spending and most especially as a way to reach the vast market of senior boomers. For the latter, indeed, the shift-to-value proposition seems ready-made, answering their needs for lower cost, expectation of quality, and comfort with innovation—in particular, with technological innovation. Those value players who can shift to value in some of the as yet underpenetrated areas of particular importance to the elderly—health care, prescription drugs, leisure, community (including housing), and financial services—may be particularly noteworthy as investment opportunities.

There's Life Left in the Old World

More than a few wags have referred to the mature economies of North America, Japan, and Western Europe as the "submerging" markets. Nonsense. Aging populations, undermaintained infrastructure, and heavy household and government debt burdens will indeed slow the overall pace of economic growth in these countries. No argument there. Developing economies can grow faster simply because they are *developing*; they are building the highways, rail lines, ports, power plants, and factories that are the basics of a modern economy and that were previously lacking. Investors, however, will do themselves a major disservice if they jump to the conclusion that profitable opportunities cannot exist where national economic growth is slow, just as they will do themselves a disservice if they neglect opportunities in places that may seem backward.

As we have seen, businesses based in highly developed economies enjoy advantages even when the growth around them slows. Experience, know-how, and access to the most advanced engineering, logistical, marketing, and financial expertise will give a competitive advantage to those developed-market companies that figure out how best to use them.

There's no crystal ball, but those enterprises that find their edge in the needs and wants of an aging population, in the premium-value-added arena, and by staking a claim to the upmarket mass market are likely to be winners in our older, slower, tiring but by no means asleep developed and still rich economies.

The Bottom Line

The developed economies still offer rich investment opportunities—specifically, in the character of their markets and in the entrepreneurial capabilities that distinguish them as developed.

Among the advantages enjoyed by mature economies are:

- Size.
- Wealth.
- Technological know-how.
- Established and (relatively) stable legal and regulatory regimes.
- Relatively sound corporate governance, reporting, and disclosure standards (note that I did say "relatively," not "perfectly").

Aging baby boomers represent a vast source of demand for health, leisure, and financial products and services as we seek to maintain physical and financial capacities over a longer life span.

Populations are aging in most countries, but the developed economies are, with some exceptions, aging most quickly. As a result, mature economies have a head start in supplying the products and services that cater to aging populations wherever they're located.

Developed economies continue to monopolize brands that carry the prestige and reputation for quality that aspiring consumers worldwide are willing to pay for.

Because powerful brands are difficult to establish and can command premium prices, they offer important profit potential. Be alert for the brand that's threatened with tarnish, however.

Companies in developed economies have perfected the premium-value-added products that are in demand among aspiring global consumers, especially consumers who have become Internet-savvy. Often these companies reside in countries like Japan that we don't always associate with rapid growth. Again, think about who is creating economic value, not where they get their mail.

The value players perfecting the shift-to-value formula, especially as the formula pertains to the increasing number of senior boomers, may offer a particularly rich vein of investment opportunity.

Chapter 7

The New Diversification: Alternatives to What?*

Wwe invest in enterprises that we think will create economic value, whether in the fast-growing emerging economies or in the more slowly growing developed economies, because that is the way to build wealth. In capitalistic systems—and increasingly in systems that would be embarrassed to be called capitalist—we participate in this value-growing phenomenon through ownership in several different forms.

Ownership might come through founding your own business—or, perhaps, through taking over your father-in-law's. It might be represented

---

*Much of the material in this chapter appeared previously in *On Wall Street* magazine, a publication of SourceMedia Inc. directed toward professional financial advisors. I am indebted to the editors for permission to reuse the material here.

in your own earnings power, as we'll talk about in more detail in Chapter 8. Or it might be exercised by owning a piece of somebody else's enterprise, by paying money to buy shares in the enterprise—and thus helping to fund its development or operations—in order to make money when those shares gain in value.

That is the simple formula for equities investing, and it remains the central way to build wealth in any economic environment—boom or bust, retrenchment or recovery. The trick is to find and invest in the enterprises that can create and over time grow that wealth-building value, and much of this book has been aimed at showing you where and how to look for such enterprises in a world that's changing before our eyes. Now we have to ask ourselves what we do when the world, or at least the stock market, doesn't choose to value those moneymaking enterprises the way it should.

Stock markets do that from time to time, which is why nobody's portfolio value just grows straight up; not even our old friend, the Great Moderation, could make that happen all the time. So "Nobody's portfolio value grows straight up all the time" is a truism on a par with "I never promised you a rose garden" and "Mama said there'd be days like this," and, like those clichés, it is indisputable; you can take it to the bank. It is frustrating but a fact that some stocks do not grow much, or do not grow consistently, or grow very nicely and then plummet to earth, or sort of just sit there even when the companies that issue the stock create real economic value.

There is no cure for this; markets are in the business of valuing future earnings, and along with every other prognosticator of the future, they do their business inconsistently, often incomprehensibly, and sometimes just wrongly. Stock prices can remain depressed—unjustifiably or not—for long periods of time. They have done so on several occasions in the not terribly distant past: from 1929 to 1953, for example, from 1968 to 1982, and for a period commencing in 1999 that as of this writing has yet to end.

All of these prolonged periods of low equities growth were rooted in political or macroeconomic causes well beyond the control of the individual investor—and well beyond his or her ability to second-guess their impact. In today's global economy, the interrelatedness of political events or macroeconomic developments has intensified; the effect of these events and developments on each other and on stock prices is more acute, often more immediate, and perhaps more profound than ever before, and the second-guessing is correspondingly even tougher.

Inflation, deflation, war, failing financial institutions that are too big to fail, and the threat of sovereign insolvency: Figuring out where they'll strike next is like playing a game of three-card monte, and your odds of guessing right are about as good as beating a sidewalk card shark.

One thing we do know about these cosmic forces: They don't have to happen in our backyard for us to be affected. Thus, in 1997, when the Thai government floated the baht in hopes of relieving its sovereign insolvency, the outward ripples triggered a slump in currencies and a devaluation of asset prices at a critical level across Asia and threatened to swamp the world's economy. The subprime mortgage collapse in the U.S. housing market similarly did not respect borders, nor did it get hung up on distance; when that bubble burst in 2007, the disastrous overflow washed thousands of miles into every economic nook and cranny on the planet.

But we can't simply come to a standstill and expect these cosmic forces to dissipate and the very down-to-earth problems they generate to go away. History teaches us that all of them—war, sovereign insolvency, deflation, inflation, even the failure of institutions too big to fail—are here to stay. Nor is there any sense in just waiting out some low point in the stock market and counting down the hours until the next high tide, which you feel sure is bound to come because, after all, good things do happen from time to time. And even those good things can have a disruptive (but not bad) impact on financial markets. The fall of the Berlin Wall in 1989, for example, delivered a peace dividend of falling defense expenditures; vast, expanding, newly free markets; and nearly a decade of solid equity returns. Less dramatically, the spring of 2009 saw the rescue strategies of global central banks take hold, the U.S. banking system prove a bit more stable than feared, and U.S. stock averages soar by nearly 65 percent by year-end. Extrapolating trends in bad times can be as costly as assuming the good times will keep rolling. I knew a retired gentleman who spent the decade of the 1980s expecting the bad old days of the previous decade to resume; he lost nearly a lifetime of savings trying to short what became a long bull market and left his heirs with a drawerful of debts.

There will be periods of slow growth, no growth, and, yes, outright declines in your equity investment portfolio. Period. In a world of advancing technology and the growing reach of prosperity, those times will pass, and those of us who own pieces of successful businesses will in due course profit. The problem, of course, aside from natural human impatience, is that while you're waiting, your basement could flood in the next tropical storm, as mine did, and you could be forced to sell those undervalued shares at depressed prices so that you can pay for the pumping, the cleaning, the new floor, the four feet of sheetrock for the bottom half of the walls, and the disposal of all that stuff you were saving for posterity. The reality of investing is that you need to own something of growing value to enjoy growing prosperity, but the timing of your needs and the market's whims may be dangerously out of sync.

The way to address that reality is through what the tech support people on your computer hotline call a work-around—in this case, alternative investments that extend the range of the portfolio and gird the equities' growth track, regardless of whether or not the equities themselves are growing in value. These alternatives might dampen the impact of inflation, cushion the blow of a sharp economic downturn, or buffer your portfolio in some way from the effects of a sovereign action like bailing out Greece or waging two wars at once. In all of these ways, they take the onus off equities to produce growth consistently, which simply is too much to ask.

You know this, of course. It's called diversification. You do it with asset classes and with individual stock picks as well, allocating your resources among a range of investment choices so that when one choice performs badly, others, performing better, can mitigate the impact— stem the loss or make up for the failure. You choose investments that don't correlate so that, as noted earlier, when one investment zigs, the other will zag.

Here's another case where we thought we had things down to a science but found out that our fancy asset-allocation tools were still assuming a flat planet Earth. Money managers used to build nine-box investment style matrices on a simplistic asset-allocation premise, as if choosing mutual funds or stocks to invest in were a game of hopscotch. The vertical axis of the matrix represented market capitalization—small-cap, mid-cap, or large-cap. The horizontal axis was valuation—value, blend, or growth funds. (See Table 7.1.) The matrix therefore contained

Table 7.1 Equity Style Boxes

	Value	Blend	Growth
Large–Cap	Large/value	Large/blend	Large/growth
Mid–Cap	Mid/value	Mid/blend	Mid/growth
Small–Cap	Small/value	Small/blend	Small/growth

nine boxes of alternatives: small/value, small/blend, small/growth; mid/value, mid/blend, mid/growth; large/value, large/blend, large/growth. You could use the nine-box style matrix for bonds, too, with credit quality on the vertical axis and maturity on the horizontal axis.

The money manager would fill each box with the appropriate funds or stock picks, and you were good to go; you hopped onto whichever boxes matched your risk appetite, aggressiveness or lack thereof, and investing attitude. Or, if you didn't want to express an opinion, you could distribute your investments among the style boxes and feel that you had achieved diversification and managed your investment risk. It was neat, an excellent tool (useful also for evaluating how money managers were doing relative to their competitors and whether they were experiencing style drift—sneaking in too many of their own investment choices and buying stocks that didn't fit within their assigned parameters). We had nice, quantifiable criteria for sorting investments, and, as long as the Great Moderation lived on, the style boxes gave us a reasonably good mix of ziggers and zaggers; the system worked just fine—until it didn't.

Instead, when the financial crisis erupted and we really needed *something* to go up, the only thing that did go up was correlation. The panicky market couldn't have cared less about our time-honored style boxes. Almost everything behaved the same. Like many other pieces of accepted investment wisdom, the nine-box style guide to asset allocation hasn't exactly been repealed, but it has morphed into still-evolving principles for adapting to a changing world of investments.

As with everything else in the current financial reality, therefore, we need a whole new way of looking at diversification and a whole new way of looking at the alternatives to equities among which you'll diversify. That's what this chapter provides. In it, we'll look at bonds, commodities, real estate, even hedge-fund-like strategies to see how they work in today's economic environment—or how to adjust our perception to make them work.

There are two key things to keep in mind, however, as we explore these alternatives. First, most of them lack the intrinsic power to grow earnings. They are insurance policies rather than wealth generators, insuring you, to the extent anything can, against market volatility. Second, there is a cost to allocating resources among these alternatives: By definition, some part of your money will always be languishing in a static or declining asset, while some option you passed up will be spinning money that is not going into your pocket. That's a sacrifice worth making, though. Think of it as one of the hidden costs of investing, the price you pay to moderate the impact of market volatility and find some growth somewhere.

Bonds

In the textbooks and in many financial-planning exercises, the first allocation decision an investor is typically asked to make is how to divvy up available funds among stocks, cash, and bonds. Stocks were supposed to provide growth, cash offered liquidity for near-term expenses, and debt investments in the form of bonds gave stability. If you got the balance right, you had a reasonable shot at realizing good returns and not losing your shirt.

Traditionally, therefore, bonds played a protective role in a portfolio. They were there to offset the big political and macroeconomic risks and were not particularly expected to generate major earnings growth. Albert Einstein may or may not have called compound interest "the eighth wonder of the world" and "the most powerful force in the universe," but regardless of whether he said it or not, bonds are wealth creators only if and when interest payments are compounding faster than inflation. Otherwise, the inflation will erode the value of a bond's real fixed-income returns, lower its price, and diminish its owner's purchasing power.

This classic view of the role of bonds dates from the experience of the Great Depression. From the beginning of 1929 through 1937, an all-equities S&P 500 portfolio lost over 30 percent, while a portfolio comprising 60 percent S&P 500 equities and 40 percent government bonds returned over 9 percent.[1] That experience articulated the protective capability of fixed-income investments; the long-term yields and the concomitant price appreciation of the bonds as those yields fell served as a hedge against economic slowdown or even recession. In fact, this 60/40 stock/bond allocation became the basis on which many investment plans have been developed ever since.

These plans worked well right through more recent periods as well. Let's say you were prescient enough to have started worrying about the looming subprime housing problem at the beginning of 2007. And let's say further that your worry prompted you to split off 40 percent from your S&P 500 equities portfolio and invest it in an index of long-term U.S. Treasury bonds.[2] Had you done so, near the end of 2011, your 60/40 portfolio would have returned 4.65 percent, while the all-equity alternative would have left you with a return of only 1.79 percent. There is the protective power of bonds writ large—not to mention the protective power of prescience.

When I talk about bonds in the context of portfolio diversification, I mean government bonds—also known as sovereign debt, debt that gets paid because the issuer can put you in jail if you don't cough up the revenues it demands (so it can pay off that debt) in the form of taxes. And while there are significant fixed-income opportunities beyond our shores, let's start with U.S. Treasury debt. I do so because, despite all the (justifiable) concerns about the nation's growing fiscal problems, Treasuries still represent an obligation of the U.S. government and are backed by that government's full faith and credit and by the Federal Reserve's ability to print all the electronic greenbacks it may choose. Given the overall strength and resiliency of the American economy, that's a good obligation to be owed. If ever the U.S. government cannot meet that obligation, it will be because of occurrences that don't bear thinking about, and chances are good that your investments will be the last thing on your mind. But for anything short of that level of catastrophe, U.S. Treasury bonds are as good a form of financial fire insurance as you can find, or at least they have been.

Why do Treasuries play this powerful defensive role in our portfolios? Let's go back to 2007 again. Sure, bonds delivered a nice, steady flow of coupon interest payments, about 4.5 percent at the time, that provided a dependable upside even as the subprime crisis loomed. To those who reinvested their coupon payments, compounding delivered even a bit more upside. But Treasuries really protected your portfolio not through the power of compound interest but through price appreciation. Yields fell during that period, and when yields fall, bond prices rise, offsetting the decline in equities. As 10-year Treasury yields fell from more than 4.5 percent at the beginning of 2007 to about 2 percent five years later, the Barclays Capital 10-year Treasury total return index, the benchmark for measuring relative bond performance, appreciated by more than 50 percent.

It's important to understand why things worked that way, because we next have to see why the protective power of Treasuries has met a dose of kryptonite. In bad economic times, we're pessimistic about how well companies can do financially and, consequently, about how fast our money can grow in relatively risky investments like stocks. Because of those concerns, we and a lot of other investors prefer to own nominally safer investments like high-quality bonds. As increased demand pushes up bond prices, we find we must accept lower and lower interest rates to buy those bonds.[3]

Here's how the math works: Second by second, the global bond markets make up their collective minds about how much yield they require to buy and sell bonds at specific coupon rates—that is, the amount of the fixed interest payment these fixed-income instruments will pay—at what specific maturities, and at what credit quality ratings. When the market decides to accept a lower yield for bonds with certain characteristics, as it has for Treasuries over the past few years, the market price of all bonds with those characteristics rises. Conversely, when the market turns around and demands higher yields, the market price falls.

So if you bought a newly issued 10-year U.S. Treasury bond in February 2007, your interest rate—"coupon" in the jargon—would have been 4.625 percent, and for every $1,000 you invested at the time,[4] the government would have been paying you $23.12 every six months ever since.

But actually, you're more fortunate than that. Happily for you, the world's bond markets decided after 2007 to accept a lower interest rate in exchange for the dependability of continuing payments from the U.S. taxpayer; by 2011, the market yield for Treasuries due in 2017 was less than 1 percent, which meant your $1,000 investment enjoyed a market value of about $1,185. By owning that bond, therefore, you might have offset a portion of the 14 percent fall the S&P 500, for example, experienced during that same period.[5]

This instance of how very high-quality bonds can offset declines in equities is no coincidence. In fact, as we'll see shortly, things haven't always worked that way. Treasuries have provided effective diversification for your stock portfolio in the past because stocks represented the world's optimism that financial conditions would get better whereas bonds represented the fear that they would not. During periods like the Great Depression or the more recent financial crisis, fear has overcome optimism and driven up the prices of bonds, while equities' prices by and large have languished.

Bonds' very success, however, contains the seeds of their own destruction, and we'd better look more closely to see this time-honored strategy's limitation in the future. To do so, let's review some history.

The day I joined the financial services industry in mid-1983, 10-year U.S. Treasury notes yielded a bit more than 11 percent. Yields peaked at 14 percent near the middle of the following year.[6] Despite some sharp reversals along the way, yields continued to decline until they reached a historic low—about 1.75 percent—in September 2011, 12.5 percentage points below their peak. You don't need a fancy bond valuation model to figure out that those yields can't fall by another 12 and a half percentage points; in fact, they can fall by only a bit more than one-tenth as much. Zero, after all, except for some technical glitches, is an absolute floor for interest rates; practically speaking, they can't be negative, although I suppose the bank could require you to give it a toaster in exchange for holding on to your money. As a result of approaching the so-called zero bound, bonds don't have anywhere near the ability to appreciate or the ability to diversify that they had during the Great Moderation and its immediate aftermath. If interest rates can't go down, bond prices can't appreciate.

Now consider Japan (see Figure 7.1). In 1990, 10-year Japanese government bonds (JGBs) yielded about 6.5 percent, and the Nikkei 225, the leading index of Japanese stocks, traded at around 32,000. By the end of 1998, the Nikkei had fallen by more than half, and JGB yields bottomed at below 1 percent. If you had invested in both markets in 1990 and held on for the next eight years,[7] your bond portfolio would have provided considerable cushion for your less fortunate equity holdings. The problem is that since 1998, the value of the Nikkei index has fallen by almost half again—to around 8,500 as of 2011—while JGB yields have, if anything, risen. This means that Japanese bond prices didn't rise as the stock market declined; they fell, too. In other words, JGBs were a fine hedge against the weakness of the Japanese stock market until they weren't. As the Japanese economy remained weak and government debt mounted, investors simply wouldn't accept JGBs with lower yields, and there wasn't much distance left for them to fall even if there had been a market for them.

Why did all this happen in Japan? Japan's chronic economic woes—its lost, deflationary decade-plus—began with a collapse of asset bubbles that undermined the financial system and saddled banks with vastly overvalued assets. Sound familiar? Troublingly so, in light of our homegrown

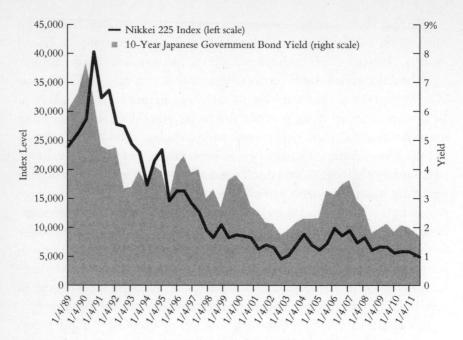

Figure 7.1 Japanese Bonds Cushioned Equity Declines Until They Didn't
SOURCE: Haver Analytics. SOURCE OF CHART DATA: Bloomberg.

American housing bubble and financial crisis. Plenty of ink has been
spilled elsewhere deciding whether the United States must follow Japan's
dismal 20-year path, and I won't add much to that speculation. Fortunately, the U.S. policy response to the economic downturn, perhaps
taking a lesson from what happened in Japan, has been far different.
In response to the financial failures of 2008, the Federal Reserve imme-
diately began creating money to buy financial assets; this quantitative
easing program was soon expanded, and the Federal Reserve's policy
making committee has promised to keep monetary conditions easy well
into the future. And where the Japanese government in 1996 attacked its
growing fiscal deficit with a significant rise in consumption taxes, the U.S.
Congress and administration have thus far refrained from doing something similar. Remember also our discussion of demographics and the
observation that while the U.S. population is aging, it remains consid-
erably younger and more dynamic than Japan's. So I refer to Japan not to
forecast another decade of equity market declines, which I don't expect,
but to emphasize that once again the former easy solutions to planning our
investments have vanished with changing times.

But put it all together—Japan's experience and our own—and keep in mind that as I write this, 10-year U.S. Treasury yields are hovering at around 2 percent, and it clarifies, I hope, the bonds situation. Simply put, they just don't have far to fall; zero's the limit. And unless you believe that the world is about to start lending Uncle Sam a trillion dollars a year for free, the realistic limit on a further decline in yields and a further spike in prices is even more limited.

Conversely, suppose the world's economic prospects brighten, making money more valuable and interest rates correspondingly higher. (Since interest is what you pay me to lend you my money, thus keeping me from spending it or buying stock with it, the more valuable money becomes, the more I will need to be paid to lend it to you.) Or suppose, even more troublingly, that inflation or credit concerns push up interest rates. Either way, as markets demand higher yields, Treasury prices have a long way to fall from their current high perch. The timeworn approach has its risks, and it has lost much of its protective power.

Finally, recall that U.S. Treasuries are not the only option for an investor looking for the diversification sovereign bonds can provide. In Chapter 5 we talked about the income-earning advantages of the bonds of emerging economies. As the Great Moderation moves south and east around the globe, the diversification value of these bonds warrants increasing attention. If bond prices can only appreciate as high yields decline, we need to look at parts of the world where yields still significantly exceed those of U.S. Treasuries.

Does the full faith and credit of the Brazilian, Turkish, or Indonesian government carry the same weight as the pledge of the U.S. government? No. But the difference has been shrinking from both directions—credit improving among the emerging sovereign nations and declining among the more mature economies like that of the United States. The repeated sovereign debt and currency crises that rocked first East Asia and then Latin America in the late 1990s and early years of the twenty-first century appear to have introduced regimens of prudent fiscal and monetary policy, and that policy has reduced the still-important risks of holding emerging-market sovereign bonds. Remember what we earlier observed about our oft-maligned neighbor to the south. The ratio of Mexico's government debt to its GDP is about half that of the United States.

Have we progressed to the point where weak economic times and slumping equity markets will dependably drive emerging-market bond yields down and bond prices up? Probably not yet, but I recall a 1985 conversation with a highly experienced Treasury bond trader who told me that given the experience of inflation in the 1970s, no one would ever buy a 30-year Treasury bond yielding less than 10 percent. We need to see a changing world more quickly than he did.

In the near term, however, should the U.S. economy slump badly, the modest protection Treasuries still offer would provide some welcome relief in a portfolio. The issue is that today, while you may want some of that protection in your portfolio, you want just enough of it and no more.

Think of bonds as fire insurance that covers a portion of your portfolio in the event a protracted bear market again threatens to burn it up. It may be annoying to pay for this coverage, but it is good to know it's there. I don't think any of us ever cursed our homeowners' insurance agent because the darn house didn't burn down before the next premium fell due. But as with any insurance policy, we need to read the fine print to be sure that we've built a bond allocation that really protects us when we need it. Remember my flooded basement.

One more issue to keep in mind: inflation. Although the wage/price spirals of the 1970s remain a distant threat to today's economy, the prices of a typical household's purchases are nevertheless increasing faster than the interest you can earn from Treasuries. When that happens, an investment in U.S. Treasuries loses purchasing power every day you own it. Overall, inflation—especially when it's worsening—is the common enemy of both bonds and equities. Although Treasuries can cushion an equity portfolio when a weak economy depresses the market's expectations of corporate earnings, during periods of persistent inflation such as many economies experienced during the 1970s, both stocks and bonds are likely to lose value. When that particular demon threatens our portfolios, we need a different kind of protection. Hard assets are an example to which we often turn.

Commodities

Commodities were once the province of farmers, Hollywood scriptwriters, and a tight club of traders wearing colorful jackets and communicating in throat-killing screams and bizarre sign language. But there is something comforting about so-called real assets like agricultural products and other raw materials that keep us fed, clothed, and sheltered and that feed the maw of industry. And then there are precious metals that are useful only for storing value or gilding anniversary presents. So it was not unexpected that once stocks began their decline, investors fled to commodity-related mutual funds. From 2006 through 2011, these funds grew from $20.8 billion in assets under management to $156 billion. That's a lot of wheat, barley, sugar, corn, cotton, cocoa, coffee, pork bellies, oil, and aluminum. To understand how commodities can strengthen a portfolio and to understand their investment limitations, we need to look at both the supply and the demand side of commodity markets.

Supply

One reason for this stampede of money into real assets is that in a world in turmoil, people fear shortages in supplies of the necessities—and food and energy top the list of necessities. Another flood, another drought, another season of upheaval in the Middle East, and worries about running out of some essential commodity intensify.

Perhaps the first and most famous of these alarms was sounded back in the nineteenth century by Thomas Malthus, an English scholar and clergyman, and an early contributor to the modern study of economics and to its reputation for being the dismal science. Malthus argued famously—or infamously—that geometrically increasing populations would inevitably overtake the earth's ability to produce enough food. We would solve that problem as famine reduced the world's population. Dismal indeed.

Our era's Malthusian fear focuses on oil. Even before the oil embargo and ensuing oil shocks of the early 1970s pushed the U.S. price of gas at the pump from 39 cents to 55 cents and finally to the unthinkably high price of $1.00 per gallon, earnest Cassandra-like worriers had warned that petroleum was on the verge of global depletion; one forecast in the mid-1950s prophesied that the last drop would be pumped around now (2012). Today's concerns about peak oil continue this debate about what logically must be a finite substance, and a similar discussion revolves around other extractive resources. In some cases—that of rare earths, for example—the worry is about limited access to a raw material seen as essential; these worries carry a political dimension and implications of national security.

The investment implications are more down-to-earth. Basically, the idea is that if we're going to run out of or be unable to get to something that everyone needs, I want to own a chunk of it for when the supply gets tight. Picture all those people lined up at the hardware store buying batteries as a hurricane approaches. If I had my own supply, I bet I could extract a pretty good markup from the people standing at the back end of the line.

The problem with the supply-side argument for investing in commodities—especially for investing in them as a way to manage risk and hedge volatility—is that supply has generally proven more flexible than worriers thought. The 2006 discovery of huge fields of pre-salt oil in Brazil, not far from the fancy beaches and favela slums of Rio de Janeiro, changed the world's petroleum picture—and gave an enormous shot in the arm to the Brazilian economy. Indeed, projections about diminishing supply haven't always held much water (another commodity that faces scarcity) because the supply at one price will be quite different from the supply at a higher price. Extraction costs of $40 a barrel, for example, make the new Brazilian pre-salt crude part of the world's oil supply at $100 a barrel, but not at $30 a barrel.

In agriculture as well, supply responds to demand. Malthus's forecast didn't anticipate the improvements in transportation and farming methods. Yet those improvements vastly increased both usable cropland and the amount of foodstuffs that could be produced on a given piece of land.

And here is where we come to the critical investment issue. Parallel to the world's increasing demand for raw materials is technology's increasing ability to innovate in ways that affect supply sufficient to meet that demand. Here's a telling example of that: In the 20-year period from 1991 to 2011, the annualized rate of return from West Texas Intermediate crude oil (WTI crude futures contract) was 8.83 percent, while the annualized total return from the equity of the oil services company Schlumberger was 11.93 percent.[8] An investor who correctly anticipated the continuing supply constraints of oil would have profited either way, but the investment returns from finding a successful innovator in accessing oil turned out better than the returns from the commodity itself. It's like the old saying about how it's better to teach someone how to fish than to give him a hunk of cod. Know-how is likely to be more valuable than the stuff it produces. We'll bring this point home in the next chapter.

Demand

Malthus thought that food shortages would lead to population decline. His equation was simple: Demand would prove self-limiting because there would be fewer surviving mouths to feed. Statistics on world population growth and on obesity belie Malthus's demand-side expectations; supply-side advances have, so far, kept us eating. And so far, even as millions around the world emerge from the poverty of subsistence agriculture, the higher demand for both food and the resources, like energy, needed to produce food appear to be sustainable. What has happened, however, is that the growing global demand, coupled with an unusual onslaught of droughts, floods, and earthquakes, has driven up the price of agricultural commodities. At times during the single year 2011, for example, the prices of wheat, corn, and soybeans had each risen by anywhere from 25 to 60 percent.[9]

As with supply, rising prices are part of the solution on the demand side, prompting innovators to figure out how to produce more and consumers to shift what they buy. In developed countries, we may drive less, switch to more energy-efficient cars, or settle for chicken at home rather than steak in a restaurant. Or, when cotton hits $2.00 a bushel, we may have to reacquire a taste for polyester. In emerging economies, the transition from subsistence agriculture to a market-based economy does not provide such easy decisions, and for both political and humanitarian reasons, we cannot expect the process to reverse. But as former Saudi oil minister Sheik Ahmed Zaki Yamani supposedly said, "The Stone Age didn't end for lack of stone."

I racked up about 125,000 air miles last year, accumulated mostly in flying around the country to address investor audiences. At some point, the combined price of airline tickets plus the less measurable costs in time and physical wear and tear will likely prompt my employer to decide that an investment in some virtual-reality technology will pay for itself by letting me attend even more of those meetings while sitting at my desk. If I knew who might provide the hardware and software that will make those virtual meetings possible, I might prefer to own their equity than the futures contracts for aviation fuel.

What does this mean for investors? Certainly, owning an interest in agricultural commodities may be a way to benefit from the growing demand. As with supply constraints, however, investors are more likely to profit from finding the enterprises that are innovating to meet the demand.

Investing in Commodities

While investing in agricultural products and essential raw materials in order to profit from relative price changes can be successful, it's a tough assignment. Tracking the market value of oil, wheat, or aluminum to catch the moment when they appreciate faster than the prices of what we consume or otherwise invest in, then selling them when they don't, is a tricky business. More usefully, in my opinion, commodities can serve to preserve wealth and purchasing power when the economy faces significant shocks.

We've already seen how in inflationary periods the prices of both stocks and bonds may suffer together. Commodities can help protect investors as the prices of everything, except stocks[10] and bonds, spiral upward. Even at times when inflation does not seem to be a clear and present danger for the United States, the risk of an inflationary surprise justifies a more or less permanent, broad-based allocation of commodities in any portfolio. If high-quality bonds can provide fire insurance to your portfolio, commodities can insure against the risk that that old burglar, inflation, will stealthily steal your purchasing power.

Commodities may also cushion your wealth from the impact of events outside the usual range of economic developments. Given what we've all seen of market and geopolitical shocks, we're quite naturally a bit gun-shy about the standard or better-known financial asset classes, about currencies, even about real estate. Rightly so, as this book has argued: Confidence in the financial verities that used to guide us is misplaced, because those verities are simply no longer verities. Commodities—real assets—offer a shock-absorption function that, in my view, is the strongest argument for adding them to your portfolio.

A case in point is what happened with oil during the Arab Spring of 2011 and, in particular, the revolution in Libya. What happened with the actual availability of oil during those events—uprising after uprising changing governments across North Africa and the Middle East—was surprisingly little, although the markets exaggerated the impact. Libya, where disruptions most directly threatened the supply, had produced 1.8 million barrels of crude on an average day before the conflict, about half the amount that Saudi Arabia can increase its daily production. During the six months of fighting that eventually ended the reign of Colonel Muammar el-Qaddafi, oil production in Libya was at a virtual standstill, although both sides in the conflict took care to preserve the oil fields as best they could. Yet the interruption of Libyan supply during the fighting was not enough, from a pure supply perspective, to cause the price of crude purchased for delivery one month later to rise more than 20 percent. The difference was risk,[11] a premium investors will pay, not because there was less actual supply or oil, but because the range of future supplies had become significantly less clear. As has been the case for almost 40 years, oil prices will no doubt rise and fall with the ongoing rhythm of political crisis and change in the Middle East oil-producing region, and an allocation to that commodity can provide one of those insurance policies that pays off should your basement flood just as Middle Eastern political tensions flare.

The headlines are not the best source of investment advice. Investors need to pay attention to what's going on in the world, but they should be cautious in translating news into buy or sell orders. Investors may profit from owning commodities if their superior insight tells them that over a given investment horizon certain commodities will appreciate faster than new supplies or attractive substitutes can come to market.

But keep in mind that commodities are financially inert and that their long-term appreciation potential is limited. A bushel of corn doesn't pay interest and can't readily be managed to enhance its earnings, while innovation and shifting demand can change its value—one way or the other—substantially. What commodities can do is maintain their market value when supply or demand shocks threaten to make them scarcer, or when inflation makes everything more costly. This property of commodities means that they perform best as investments when other holdings—stocks, bonds, real estate—go into a slump. Thus their role as theft insurance: own them in case trouble intrudes, but don't complain if they prove unnecessary.

Gold

Gold's appreciation by more than 450 percent in the 10-year period from 2001 to 2011 provides another example of commodities' response to increasing risk. Gold tends to zig when other financial assets zag, and investors typically turn to gold when other markets are slumping.

In my view, however, the stunning rise in the value of gold in the first decade of the twenty-first century should really be attributed to concerns about the long-term exchange value of paper currencies, especially the dollar. I think so for at least two reasons. First, the 10-year rise did not reflect a contemporaneous rise in the nominal prices of the goods and services we buy and use; in fact, prices almost deflated during that time period. Second, the size of gold's appreciation in dollars was not matched in other currencies during that decade. While the price of gold in euros and yen did increase from 2001 to 2011—by 223 percent in the euro and by 257 percent in yen—the rise was nowhere near the 450 percent appreciation in the dollar price.

So what the huge appreciation in the value of gold tells us is that investor confidence in monetary policy has frayed. In the flight from paper currencies, precious metals become a refuge.

In fact, investors should think of gold more as a currency than as a commodity. Currencies store the value that we create on the job or through our investments. We accept dollars as pay for our labor because we can eventually exchange those dollars for goods and services. A riskier, more uncertain world, however, raises doubts about how much our dollars will actually buy some time in the future. Those doubts might prompt me to exchange some of my dollars for another sovereign currency, but if the doubts about an uncertain world also have me concerned about the backing for the euro, yen, or real, I might use the alchemy of commodity markets to turn the dross of paper currency into gold, which no government can debase by printing.

Like that bushel of corn, however, a gold bar is financially inert. It pays no interest, produces no earnings, and does not have a business plan. It is simply a hedge against inflation, monetary debasement, and in particular against volatility and uncertainty. But without doubt, as a tool of managing risk in an uncertain world, it shines.

Real Estate

In practice, real estate doesn't belong in a discussion of alternative asset classes. There's nothing alternative about the house we live in, which constitutes a core investment—maybe the sole investment—of many households. Owning a home has been both the literal and figurative foundation of the American dream, providing not just shelter but financial security and a dependable way to build wealth. Politicians bragged as U.S. home ownership rates reached all-time highs in the mid-2000s. And any investment that came close to a home in terms of financial dependability was dubbed "safe as houses."

The phenomenon is neither new nor uniquely American. I recall a British politician telling me in the early 1970s that when a sufficient number of British families owned their own homes, "the country will be safe from Communism." A nineteenth-century commentator even blamed the American Civil War on low levels of home ownership in the South.[12] No wonder the recent decline of some 30 percent in housing prices left so many of us stunned.

Once you allow for inflation, however, home ownership has rarely been a great investment, especially compared to the stock market. Yale economist Robert Shiller has re-created very long-term investment results for the U.S. equity and housing markets and for consumer inflation. His results are sobering, as you can see in Figure 7.2. Over the past 120 years in the United States, there was only one period—the post–World War II years—during which house prices moved up faster than inflation and *stayed there* for more than a short time. That period may be explained by the early baby boomers pushing up their parents' need for more housing, by stepped-up subsidization of home purchases, and by suburbanization tempting cramped apartment dwellers into more expensive single-family housing. In any event, the circumstances and the robustness of housing prices are not likely to be soon repeated.

Allowing for inflation does somewhat miss the point of real estate investments, including one's own home. At least home prices kept up

Figure 7.2   Home and Equity Markets, 1890–2010
SOURCE OF CHART DATA: Robert J. Shiller.

with inflation during periods like the 1970s when real, inflation-adjusted returns on stocks and especially bonds declined. That's key, because if you can't at least keep up with inflation, you're getting poorer with every breath you take. Real estate beat stocks and bonds during the 1970s because each piece of real estate has an actual or (as with your house) an implied rent. Rents, even implied rents, can be raised. Since a parcel of real estate is worth today's estimated value of total future (implied) rental income, and since, during periods of inflation, landlords can raise rents in tune with the overall consumer market basket—something bond-holders and many other businesses cannot do—real estate holds its value reasonably well when inflation strikes. Owning a house, therefore, makes a reasonably good hedge against inflation returning to plague us once again.

But just recognizing its inflation-fighting power is to underestimate the importance of home ownership in building our wealth. At the end of the third quarter of 2011, owner-occupied housing accounted for more than 28 percent of household net worth, although that was down from 35 percent at the end of 2006.[13] Home ownership helped build families' wealth, however, less because of *what* we owned than because of *how* we owned it. It worked well for many us because the long-term mortgage that typically financed our home purchase afforded us two financial advantages we might not have been aware of. First, the scheduled principal repayments hidden in our monthly mortgage pay-ment forced us to save regularly, taking an increasing amount out of consumption each month and adding to our home equity. And as we have already seen, the average American household wasn't saving in any other way. Second, borrowing 80 percent or more of the price allowed us to buy on margin, providing the only access to financial leverage that most of us could probably obtain and amplifying our profits while markets rose. And don't forget that, unlike the stocks and bonds in your portfolio, your house provided a place to live that you didn't otherwise have to pay someone else for. Put those factors together, and the role homes have played in our financial planning becomes a lot less surprising.

But we can all feel that last dip in the housing-price roller coaster. From the end of 2006 through the third quarter of 2011, owner-occupied home values declined by almost $6.6 trillion, or by about 43 percent of the total amount of goods and services the United States produced in the preceding year. The housing market created a huge asset bubble, a lot like the tulip bubble of 1637, the South Sea Company bubble of 1711, the 1920s stock market bubble, and plenty more similar bubbles from the darker annals of economic history. We all feel it, but while politicians and protestors all look for someone to blame, our job is to look ahead.

Personally, I've always thought of my home as something like my car. I buy it, I use it, and if I take reasonably good care of it, someone may buy it from me when it no longer serves my purpose. Unlike my cars, which I pretty much drive until no one will want them, there's a good chance that the resale of my house will net me a bit more than the rate of inflation while I owned the place. I don't expect it to make me rich, and if it does appreciate in value, only a dire financial emergency would get me to draw on a home equity line, much less use it as an ATM machine as in days of yore.

Hedge Funds

Many people—maybe most people—think of hedge funds as high-risk, speculative playgrounds for gazillionaires that sometimes deliver great returns that we mere mortals can only dream about—and sometimes collapse spectacularly.[14] As with many unfamiliar matters, the daily reality is a lot duller than the periodic headlines. Hedge funds have become a routine component of many institutional portfolios and have become increasingly available to an expanding universe of individuals. They are a part of how the world of investing is changing, and for that reason alone, we all have to pay at least some attention.

Generalizing about hedge funds is like generalizing about investment books. Are they all worth owning? No. Do they differ greatly in their approach? Yes. Can any one of them solve all your financial problems? No, not even this one. But because many hedge funds attempt to provide a continuous, stable return across all market conditions, hedge fund techniques, when executed successfully, can provide investors with a narrower range of investment outcomes during volatile periods. Figure 7.3 compares the (price) return of our familiar S&P 500 equity index with the Dow Jones Credit Suisse Hedge Fund Index since the beginning of the financial mess in 2007. Note that there's nothing to choose from until times get tough in late 2007, after which the hedge fund index does a better job of holding its value than does the stock

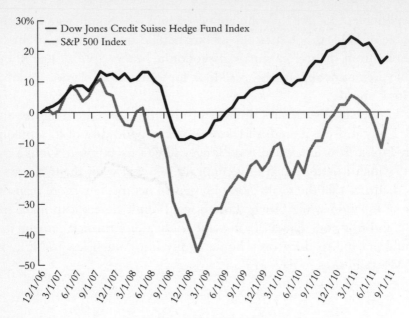

Figure 7.3   Hedge Fund Performance versus Equities, 2006–2011

Source: Dow Jones Indexes and Credit Suisse Index Co., LLC. Source of chart data: Bloomberg. © CME Group Index Services LLC, 2012.

index. Note, however, that the stock index also proved more volatile—now in a good way—when financial markets recovered strongly in the spring of 2009 and the fall of 2011.

The difference was even more pronounced during the long equity bull market of the 1990s, as shown in Figure 7.4. Hedging mutes returns, both when you want it to and when you wish it didn't. Such is the nature of hedging your position. Insurance against loss always comes at a price.

What are the secret ingredients of hedge funds? The principal ones include the ability to short securities—selling something you don't currently own with the expectation of buying it later at a lower price; the use of leverage or borrowing to amplify the modest profits to be made from many small transactions (and losses when those investments disappoint); the use of options, swaps, and other derivatives to seek the returns of markets the manager cannot access directly; and the ability to invest without restraint in whatever the manager may find to add value. Of at least as much importance as their investing techniques, hedge fund sponsors typically limit both when and how much investors can

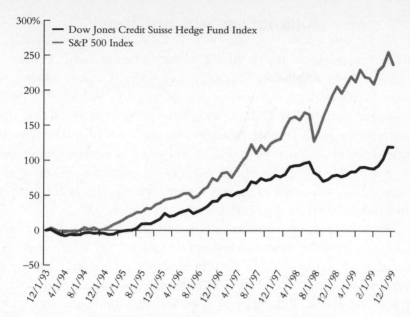

Figure 7.4   Hedge Fund Performance versus Equities, 1993–2000

SOURCE: Dow Jones Indexes and Credit Suisse Index Co., LLC. SOURCE OF CHART DATA: Bloomberg. © CME Group Index Services LLC, 2012.

contribute to the fund and when and how much they can withdraw. These limitations allow the manager to hold illiquid positions without fear of having to return cash at a bad time; they also protect the manager—and existing investors—from a flood of new cash arriving at a particularly inopportune time.

One other feature of hedge funds merits mention, a place where hedge funds and investment books part company: Hedge funds tend to be quite expensive. Typically, hedge fund managers charge basic management fees larger than a mutual fund would charge and then collect an additional fee for performance that exceeds a specified benchmark.

For cost and other reasons, including federal regulatory restrictions on who qualifies to buy into such a fund, hedge funds aren't for every investor. But even investors who won't go near actual hedge funds need some familiarity with the techniques, their risks, and their advantages, because conventional mutual fund managers are finding some of these hedging techniques useful in achieving their more limited mandates. Read your disclosure statements and ask questions if they seem unfamiliar.

Alternatives Are Just That

Let's remember what we're talking about with the term *alternatives*. It means other possibilities. That's all. Specifically, it means other possibilities in addition to equities, which still need to be the core of an investment portfolio aimed at growing your prosperity. You'll find that growth in the kinds of enterprises and in the kinds of markets we've talked about in the previous chapters, and you can buttress and defend that growth by diversifying into the other possibilities. They're the insurance, but you need to own a house—the equities at the core of your portfolio—before you buy the insurance on it.

The other possibilities serve a range of purposes. Some may help your equity portfolio offset macroeconomic forces over which you have no control, or serve as shock absorbers against such risks. Others can appreciate in value even during inflation or serve as a hedge against market fluctuations. Put them all together, and they constitute some level of protection against unpredictable eventualities.

You have a better shot at finding the right alternatives for your prosperity goals if you have some sense of what those unpredictable eventualities may bring—if you can know the risks you're offsetting or against which you need a shock absorber. That's not easy to do. Take the euro as an example. Until recently the common European currency vied with the U.S. dollar for a role in global financial reserves. Remember the supermodel who demanded to be paid in euros rather than dollars? But as I write these words, I can't tell you with any certainty that the euro will exist in its current form a year from now. Nor can I predict what it will mean if it does not exist. We do know this: Fires will break out in this universe of uncertainties, and burglars may be lurking in the shadows. Insurance across a range of alternatives can play a significant role in keeping your prosperity growing.

The Bottom Line

Like everything else in the new financial reality, diversification needs to be redefined. Traditional categories of asset classes have failed to provide the diversification benefit many of us expected. So-called alternatives can play a new role in portfolio diversification.

Before considering an alternative asset class, ask what it's an alternative to. The answer should be equities. Alternatives to equities can serve as insurance or a hedge against:

- Inflation.
- Economic weakness.
- Disruptive global events.
- Currency debasement.
- The need to liquidate a long-term holding to meet a financial emergency or opportunity.

U.S. Treasuries have lost much of their protective power but remain important fire insurance against a protracted decline in the overall economy or in the equity market. Bonds of other sovereignties may be able to supplement U.S. Treasuries in that role.

Investing in commodities requires tracking both supply and demand and can be a tough assignment, but commodities can serve as a shock absorber in a diverse portfolio. A traditional store of value, gold can be insurance against economic slumps. Your home has value as a place to live and as a hedge against inflation. Your home is unlikely to provide investment returns much beyond inflation, however, and should never be treated as if it were an ATM.

Hedge fund investing is an expensive but potentially valuable way to find stability in shifting market conditions.

Chapter 8

Investing in Human Capital—Yours

What are you worth?

I don't mean your material assets—house, car, possessions, bank account, stock portfolio, art on the walls, skis/bikes/ sailboat in the garage. I mean you: If you were an investment, how would you assess your economic value? What, exactly, is the amount of that economic value—what I'll call your accumulated human capital?

In theory, the value of any investment is simply the earnings it can produce in the future translated into today's money—discounted present value.[1] Think of your own value in the same way: Given that you are an investment of which you are the 100 percent owner, the economic value of that investment—and, therefore, the measure of your financial worth—equals the discounted present value of your future earnings. To illustrate, I'll make it personal: My friends and family value me for my evident wit and pleasing personality, but the firm that employs me values me for my work, and it's the firm that gives me cash

145

every two weeks. My value, therefore, is an amount the firm has determined it realizes as a return on the work I do. And please don't tell them otherwise.

How does accumulated human capital work in life? Suppose you want an income of $10,000 a month for the next 30 years. How much capital would that require? How much would you need to invest today to pay yourself 10 grand a month out of principal and interest, accepting that you'll have a zero balance 30 years from now? At 3 percent interest, which is the rate on 30-year U.S. Treasury bonds as I write this, and with the assurance that the monthly $10,000 payment will cease after 30 years, the answer is $2,371,893.82. If instead of buying an income-producing investment, you figure on earning $10,000 a month for the next 30 years, you've just figured out today's value of what is likely to be your most valuable asset—you—if the asset continues to work productively for the next 30 years.

You may never have thought of yourself as capital captured in protoplasm, but you are, and $2.37 million is a big number by just about any measure. But it is probably not big enough. Not when you factor in other inevitable realities.

Inflation is the first of those realities. Ten thousand dollars a month may seem like a comfortable income. After all, it's about twice the median household income for American households—at least as of about 2009. Remember, however, that we're concerned with purchasing power, not just with a bunch of numbers, and that's where inflation and its tendency to crush purchasing power come in. Let's figure a rate of just 2 percent in annual price increases for all the goods and services you're going to buy over those three decades. That is a generous assumption because for most of those years inflation will likely be higher than 2 percent, but let's go with it for the moment. When we factor that modest amount of inflation into the equation, your $10,000 per month buys less and less with each passing year until, 30 years from now, it is buying today's equivalent of only $5,400. And that's the best-case scenario; the inflation rate, to repeat, is unlikely to remain as low as 2 percent for 30 years.

So inflation is a key reason the $2.37 million is probably not a big enough number—especially since, after all, you're hoping to see your standard of living increase, not fall. For that, you're going to need, as the saying goes, a bigger boat. In fact, maintaining just a steady-state purchasing power equivalent of $10,000 per month for 30 years will require, given even minimal inflation, a good deal more than $2.37 million; it is going to take a much, much bigger investment. Actually, just getting to $12,000 per month means you'd need to be worth an extra half million *now*.

Moreover, you are going to want to save some of that $10,000 per month. You will want a cushion against family emergencies, natural disasters, all the vagaries of global macroeconomic dynamics, and such unforeseen events as sudden disability, sudden unemployment, or the slightly less sudden appearance of triplets in the family—anything that may cause you to deplete your principal or default on future payments. So add to the investment of $2.37 million a realistic amount of savings to serve as a contingency reserve, or you'd better start drawing down rather less than that comfortable $10,000.

And unless you want to end up working as a greeter in a discount retail mall or taking orders at an instant oil-change emporium into your sixties, seventies, and maybe even beyond, you'll need to have some financial capital saved up to produce income when your human capital has grown tired of doing so. The ideas developed in the rest of this book aim to help you grow that financial capital, but there won't be any financial capital at all unless your earning power exceeds your spending proclivities. The moral of the story is to therefore take another cut out of that monthly income to invest in other people's ability to generate value, or better yet, start figuring out how to increase the value of your human capital right now. Or best, do some of both.

Inflation, contingencies, savings, and investments for future needs: What amount of current investment are you up to by now? My guess is that the $2.37 million has evolved into a much higher amount, driven by a more realistic and much larger expectation for the present value you need to achieve for your accumulated human capital. How will you earn that higher amount?

The question is fundamental. We all tend to forget that, unless we've already amassed a fortune or inherited someone else's, our biggest investment position is ourselves. That has always been the case, but prior to the financial crisis and the global recession, it was more likely to have been accepted in the abstract rather than regarded as a tangible asset that must be managed actively. Like so many matters we've discussed, the old way won't work anymore.

With traditional industries at best evolving in substantive ways, at worst simply going the way of the dinosaur, and with new industries requiring unprecedented kinds of skills and capabilities, nothing that we grew up with during the years of the Great Moderation remains sacred. All those assumptions we received about work and careers—like "Put in your 40 years in a good company and retire with a gold watch and a good pension," or "You can always be a teacher," or "A government job is safe," or "You'll make top dollar right out of law school," or (if you're old enough to remember times deservedly behind us), "A girl can always get by if she knows how to type"—have all been tarnished. Everything is up for grabs—in the world of work and in the world of finance.

Whether we like it or not, part of accepting the world as it is and not as we'd like it to be is to find new ways to transfer our own human capital into financial capital. Don't despair: Compared to the other investments we've considered, this is the one you can control. True, everything from the evolving global economy to the strategic decisions your employer makes will *influence* the value of your human capital, but rebuilding, maintaining, and augmenting your own value is far more within your control than is the value of anything else in your portfolio. This chapter is about how to do it.

Stocking Up on Your Human Capital

Human capital is a phrase that is thrown around a lot, meaning just about whatever the thrower likes. Let's keep it simple and clear and define it as the inherent or acquired abilities each one of us possesses—knowledge, skills, natural talents, and the experience that adds to or refines all of those things. Employers prize human capital because more and better knowledge, skills, talents, and experience among employees augment profits. Entrepreneurs succeed because they've figured out how to make or do something others value and because they've developed sufficient confidence in their ability to face the risks of the market; figuring things out and having confidence in your abilities is part of the entrepreneur's human capital. Societies believe that they flourish qualitatively as well as quantitatively when inhabitants' human capital is developed through education, health, and economic opportunity. Ergo, it is desirable, practical, efficacious, and an all-around good idea to invest in human capital—specifically, yours. And if you are going to prosper from what you can't change, developing your own human capital may be the thing that makes the difference—that holds the investment edge.

In Charlie Chaplin's movie, *Modern Times*, there's a famous scene of Chaplin with a monkey wrench in each hand turning a nut on an endless flow of unidentifiable widgets coming down an assembly line. A gaggle of dark-suited managers try to cook up ways to get Charlie to work faster and faster until the whole mess crashes. If you haven't seen this classic film, please do, but there's a point beyond Chaplin's depiction of alienated labor, a point that might abrade his political views. There's a reason those suits made more money than the Charlie character on the assembly line, and it's the same reason that Chaplin doubtless enjoyed a more comfortable life than his characters. The fat cats had skills (or so someone thought) to make many Charlies make many more widgets. Similarly, Chaplin himself had the talent and the creativity to sell movie tickets to vast audiences. The human capital of the managers and Chaplin, however they obtained it, exceeded that of the benighted worker with the monkey wrenches.

Some recent studies seem to confirm that the rising generation of educated professionals has taken this lesson to heart, although for most, the reason is that they have been traumatized by the market volatility that has followed the 2007–2008 financial crisis. A 2011 survey by MFS Investment Management found that fully a third of the portfolios of investors in their twenties was in readily accessible cash equivalents; that proportion is well above the average among all adults and seems a clear revulsion away from investing in equities. Moreover, 52 percent of these "young and riskless," as a *Wall Street Journal* article dubbed them, asserted they would "never feel comfortable" investing in stocks.[2] A study by the Investment Company Institute confirmed this reluctance to risk, finding that a mere 31 percent of investors under the age of 35 "were willing to take above-average investment risk."[3] What are these young professionals relying on instead for their prosperity? They are looking ahead to their own income-producing potential, investing in their own human capital to realize a prosperity advantage. At least they'd better.

You, too. Your human capital is not just within your control; it's also your responsibility. It's up to you to invest in your human capital as a way to gain a prosperity advantage—a way to establish an edge that enhances your economic value. The formula is simple: By building, maintaining, and modernizing your skills and capabilities, you can add to your human capital and thus have the means to increase your financial capital. This is especially important if you haven't accumulated enough cash to build the financial kind—that is, if you're not yet worth the $2.37 million-plus that will let you draw down 10 thou a month for 30 years, or achieve your own personal version of that.

But if the formula is simple, its execution is nevertheless challenging. For the bad news is that many of the same forces of global change that have shuffled the deck for stocks and bonds have shuffled the deck for human capital as well, presenting you with the challenges of rising international competition and rapid technological change. These days, even if you're a techie, you are up against not just the other graduates in your college engineering class, but also the graduates of India's Institutes of Technology and of Zhejiang University of Technology in China, as well as the kids in that garage in Silicon Valley who never bothered with college at all. You aren't just up against other individuals, either; you are competing against rising standards of innovation, changing technical processes, and new methods of wealth creation. If you are not a techie, you are up against the techies in addition to everybody else and on top of all those changing standards, processes, and methods.

The good news, however, is that if you live in a highly advanced society like ours, you have ready access to an extraordinary array of human capital development opportunities. (If you don't live in a society with such access, you can be pretty sure the access is improving and will be ready soon enough.) The even better news is that no matter where you happen to live, you have access via a range of telecommunications modalities to much of the world's intellectual and technical potential just by logging on and being self-directed. Up to now, we've talked about how you can make your financial capital grow by investing in where the new global financial potential is. By the same token, you can make your human capital grow—and thereby further augment your financial prosperity—by investing in where the human potential now is.

I'll suggest two ways to do that—through education and self-branding. I know: Both are clichés. But like all clichés, they hold a germ of truth within them, and like most things these days, they have taken on fresh meaning anyway.

Start with the installation found between your ears and the education you will need to keep it fit, sharp, and capable of helping you prosper.

Getting Educated for the Knowledge Economy

Knowledge economy is another of those terms that get thrown around a lot. We don't have to parse it too finely, however, to understand that it speaks to a fundamental shift in what drives global economic activity. For millennia, that activity was driven by agriculture. Then came the industrial economy. It segued into a service-driven economy. And we are now becoming an information-based economy, one in which knowledge is both the tool of economic activity and its product.

Certainly, there will always be a need for manual labor of one form or another; likewise, there will always be room for material products. At least, I think so. I can't quite picture a pair of postindustrial shoes, but I suppose I could be wrong. Had I thought about it, I probably would not have been able to imagine the vinyl LP giving way to the cassette, CD, and DVD, which themselves yielded in what seemed a nanosecond of time to the MP3 and the Windows Media Audio (WMA) file. Long-playing turned out to be fairly short. And speaking of short-playing products, let's talk about those shoes. I am personally acquainted with more than one individual for whom last season's Jimmy Choos have about the same value as a scratched-up 78 rpm record.

I hear that vinyl is back and that Jimmy Choo is moving big-time into China, but the truth is that the world today runs on digitally expressed data—information, knowledge, intelligence, details, facts, statistics, concepts, formulas, theses, and all the rest of it—and mastery of the tools, processes, and logistics of digital data creation, management, manipulation, and communication is essential for full participation in the current and future global economy.

That requires education. There's no doubt about the correlation between education and earnings; it is direct and straightforward. We saw it first in the early 1980s; discrepancies in real hourly wages began to veer wildly by education, with the wages of high school dropouts and even high school graduates plummeting significantly, while the earnings of college graduates and those with advanced degrees soared.[4] The discrepancies followed in part from the rising use of technologies that literally changed the nature of work and the skills needed to perform the work. In part, the discrepancies resulted from globalization, which, among other effects, vastly expanded the supply of less skilled workers and drove down wages for workers like Chaplin's nameless character, workers who simply lack the skills industries need and who therefore simply cannot compete in the marketplace.

The situation has become standard in the three decades since that time. Today's unemployment rate for college graduates, trained in the skills that enable them to compete, is about 4 percent, less than half the 9 percent rate the overall labor force suffers. Among high school dropouts, unemployment is half again the overall rate. Education simply means earnings. According to the U.S. Census Bureau's 2011 report, *The Big Payoff: Educational Attainment and Synthetic Estimates of Work-Life Earnings*, the higher the educational degree, the higher the income, with professional degrees raking in the most dollars. Table 8.1 shows how it breaks down.

Education makes the difference even at the low end of this evolving knowledge-based economy, where menial or minimally skilled jobs no less than sophisticated work will require a basic level of digital literacy and the ability to enter and update data. Trained for competency in both print and digital literacy, workers can undertake the essential jobs of tagging social media, captioning videos, scanning and verifying receipts, and continually revising existing databases. In many ways, the knowledge economy can be a great boon to these workers. All it takes is an Internet connection. The work that is needed—and therefore the jobs to be performed—are no longer dependent on roads or shipping schedules or wires or even language, although English is already becoming the lingua franca of the knowledge economy. Educated in these basics, minimally skilled workers everywhere may be able to plug

Table 8.1　　Annual Earnings by Level of Education

Education	Median Earnings
None to 8th grade	$10,271
9th to 12th grade	$10,996
High school graduate	$21,569
Some college	$27,361
Associate's degree	$32,602
Bachelor's degree	$42,783
Master's degree	$53,716
Professional degree	$73,977
Doctorate	$73,575

Source: Tiffany Julian and Robert Kominski, "Education and Synthetic Work-Life Earnings Estimates," *American Community Survey Reports*, U.S. Census Bureau, September 2011, 3.

into the knowledge economy and begin to raise their standard of living and their quality of life.

The proliferation of a basic knowledge-based economy explains much of the proliferation of wealth creation we've talked about, but the higher-level work in the knowledge economy, the kind of work that creates the wealth and rewards its creation, requires a level of erudition in a particular body of learning and a set of intellectual capabilities that are really quite particular to the demands of the economy. Specifically, it requires an understanding of what have come to be known as the STEM disciplines—science, technology, engineering, mathematics—and proficiency in critical thinking, analysis, and problem solving, along with the ability to communicate with clarity and confidence. It also goes without saying that digital literacy—indeed, fluency in digital media—will be a sine qua non of successful participation in the knowledge economy.

We know that this is already the case. Whether your particular perspective or political inclination identifies teachers' unions, funding levels, or overemphasis on educationally questionable standardized testing as the source of declining educational achievement, American students' mediocre performance in the STEM disciplines arguably dooms our students and the nation as a whole to falling behind economically. Our kids will simply lack the skills that enable them to compete—with one another and with the rest of the world. If you want to raise the value of your human capital, you'd better not be one of those kids—whatever your age.

Because the international comparisons that report the dismal state of U.S. educational achievements generally rank Asian students among the world's most successful—especially in the STEM disciplines—many commentators argue for the discipline and hard work that we think characterize Asian educational systems. Beyond a doubt, successfully investing in your human capital demands that you do better than the average American in learning these technical skills, but doing so won't be enough.

Noted journalist Fareed Zakaria, one of the more insightful among the new journalists who constitute a subset of knowledge economy practitioners, contrasted his Asian secondary education with the demands of his U.S. university education. The former, he said, gave him "an impressive base of knowledge and taught me how to study hard and fast." The latter, however, educated him in "how to solve problems, truly understand the material, question authority, think for yourself and be creative." Zakaria argues that these educational values "are why the U.S. has been able to maintain an edge in creative industries and innovation in general."[5] The STEM subjects contribute mightily to these educational values, but I'd argue that you really learn them by immersing yourself in the now-disdained curriculum of the liberal arts.

I heard a popular business television commentator remark that the disaffected students who are complaining about their lousy job prospects should have known better than to "major in English lit in the first place." He was shortsighted. Some unemployed young folks may have defective human capital and may have ducked the hard courses, but if Zakaria is correct, studying the humanities can be part of the solution, not the essence of the problem. The abilities to think analytically about what you've learned, to research subjects you don't know about, to put learning into context, and to speak and write clearly and persuasively are essential for participation in the new world of work, and they become more and more essential as the work grows more and more demanding. In fact, CEOs *expect* candidates for hire to be grounded in the subject matter of today's jobs—or to be able to acquire the technical skills through training—but what they really *prize* in a candidate are these broader intellectual qualities.

Consider some examples from highly technical industries. Lockheed Martin CEO Norm Augustine argued in a *Wall Street Journal* op-ed piece in 2011 that the study of history was "crucial" to gaining employment and succeeding in an organization—even, or perhaps especially, in one like Lockheed Martin composed primarily of engineers. Augustine fixed on history in particular because, he contended, the study of how we got to be who we are "can create critical thinkers who can digest, analyze, and synthesize information and articulate their findings,"[6] precisely the skills that distinguish those who advance in an organization in the knowledge economy from those who are merely competent in its basic skills.

At an economic policy conference in late 2011, I met a senior executive from a global mining company. His formal educational training was as a mining engineer, although he admitted that he wasn't a particularly good engineer. Instead, he is now the boss of many presumably better technicians because he had developed the ability to identify, analyze, and execute complex business strategies for exploiting markets for the stuff his subordinates dug out of the ground. Learning to be a great engineer certainly represents a sound investment in your human capital, but adding creativity to that technical base can turn a sound investment into a brilliant one. A propos, I note that STEM-heavy Singapore is now launching, in partnership with a major U.S. institution, a new university dedicated to the liberal arts.

I'm probably stretching the point a bit to suggest that simply having technical skills can make you a twenty-first-century version of Chaplin's wrench turner, but it's the broader, analytical skills that allow you to take charge of how those nuts will be turned. Becoming the kind of critical thinker that Norm Augustine looks for allows you to adapt both to a rapidly changing world and to your own view of your position in that world.

My own educational background is possibly also a case in point, and no one is more surprised by that than I am. It would be inaccurate to say that when I entered college, the world of investment management was far from my mind. The fact is that investment management wasn't even on my radar screen; I'm not even sure I knew such a profession existed. I majored in political science at the University of Chicago, still rooted in the Great Books curriculum, in the focus on primary sources, and in requiring writing—a lot of writing. So I had to read and write widely in subjects outside my major, which forced me, now that I look back on it, to learn how to learn.

In graduate school at Yale, I concentrated on urban development politics, as it was then known, and wrote a doctoral thesis based on research I carried out in Birmingham, England, and in Lyon, France. The research required me (okay, gave me an excuse) to spend a protracted period of time in two cultures that were not my own, as broadening an experience as the cliché says it is. Moreover, in the case of Lyon, it also of course required me to learn a foreign language—well enough, at least, to interview in it and understand the answers I was getting. No question that these things stretch the mind.

My objective in doing all this—in fact my goal since high school—was to teach political science at a major university, and I managed to do so, first at the University of Illinois–Chicago, and then at Princeton University. To my surprise and dismay, I found teaching at the university level deeply unsatisfying—you really ought not to teach until you know something—and I began to look around for some other kind of career.

What came up was something radically different: My academic expertise in urban finance turned out to be a pathway into the municipal bond research department of Merrill Lynch. My manager there would have been happy for me to crank out spreadsheets, which really were spread-out sheets of paper at the time, tallying municipal debt statistics, but I noticed that the people having the most fun—and making the most money—were the people who used my calculations to develop investment ideas. Thucydides didn't have much to say about the debt-service capabilities of the Athenian polis, but studying history, scientific method, and literature had taught me how to ask the right questions and build the right arguments to begin to succeed in a technical field I knew little about.

Knowing what you don't know is fundamental to investing in your human capital, and I had a great deal to learn about securities analysis, accounting, and portfolio construction. I spent dozens of weekends over three years holed up in my basement mastering the Chartered Financial Analyst curriculum, and I was never shy about asking my colleagues to share the benefits of their more traditional educational paths. So while nothing in my earlier education would ever have signaled a career as an investment professional, what my educational foundation thankfully provided instead was a grounding in essential intellectual skills and the know-how to find out what I didn't know. What mostly remained for me to do after the radical change, therefore, was to make my way up the knowledge curve on economics and investing. I'm not saying it was easy, but it was eminently possible.

By the way, it's perhaps instructive to add that right now, the head of equities at my firm is an individual who majored in geography in college, while his boss, the chief investment officer, studied Slavic languages and literature. This is probably why, when people on the rise in my organization ask me what finance textbook I think they should read next, I direct them instead to *War and Peace*, as good a "textbook" as there is about the dynamics of power, human relationships, the fundamental forces that drive people's behavior, and how the world works. If you get all that down, you'll have some excellent insights into investing. Oh, and along the way, you'd better figure out how to calculate discounted present value and be sure you have the right technical skills to evaluate, with sharp skepticism, the next complex derivative someone wants to sell you. The imperative to invest in your human capital, focusing both on the detailed technical side and on the creative, critical-thinking side, never ends.

Making Education for the Knowledge Economy Pay

Once you have invested in the essential learning in relevant subject matter and overall context and have sharpened your mind to a fine point of critical keenness and problem-solving acuity, how will you turn that education investment into a competitive edge that will raise your economic worth?

One thing is for sure: You can't stop educating yourself. Ever. You will need to apply your learning and intellectual capabilities every day to stay tuned to what is happening in the economy, in technology, in the arts, even in politics. Human capital is not a buy-and-hold investment; it's more like an investment in good Nebraska cropland. The returns depend on how diligently, consistently, and creatively you nurture it. Without constant analysis of the world and of what it demands of you, harvests will shrink. With proper cultivation, the skills and capabilities you've invested in as your human capital might well grow into returns well beyond what you now imagine.

I channeled my municipal finance know-how into an industry that just happened to be hitting an enormous growth spurt. I was lucky, both because the financial industry grew and took me with it and because when I say "channeled," I really mean "stumbled upon." My advice would be to bring a lot more forethought to your own channeling and not to rely on luck. In other words, try not to depend on stumbling into something, but be prepared if it happens.

There really are so many ways to make a living in this global, knowledge-based, wired economy. For guidance, let me suggest looking to those companies that are succeeding. Check out the enterprises that are growing in this economy, and try to identify the attributes that are propelling the growth. Are the companies international in scope or focused domestically? Either way, why? Are they reaching out to new kinds of markets? If so, which markets? Have they developed a product or service people can't get anywhere else? What is it about the product or service that makes it so desirable and so hard to come by? Have they developed brands that people trust and value? Are they managing and deploying their capital successfully, taking risks but managing those risks prudently?

You would want to invest in the equity of companies that can give the right answers to those questions. You would invest in such companies because their long-term ability to generate and grow their earnings means that their market value is likely to increase.

But there's another way in which such companies can help you grow your own market value: Do what they do. Be guided by what propels the growth of their financial capital to map the growth of your human capital.

Brand Yourself

Specifically, that means developing your brand and identifying the market it can most profitably serve. You need to define, realistically and clearly, just what your distinctive human capital consists of—your particular inherent or acquired abilities, skills, talents, expertise, and experience—and to determine the market or audience or environment that needs what you have, and to measure its dimensions. The key is in the word *distinctive* (there's that competitive edge idea again), and your human capital becomes distinctive because it is different or because it is better, or both. In other words, if your human capital is much like everybody else's human capital, you will need to enhance it or improve it in order to increase your economic value.

You do that through the continuing education process I've discussed—consistently building up your intellectual property—and, at the same time, by being first or most interesting or loudest into the marketplace. In other words, don't keep your human capital a secret while you are polishing it; if no one knows about it, it simply won't grow. And neither will the prosperity it can achieve.

I am not qualified as a career counselor or human resources professional, and this is not a career development handbook. But the shelves of bookstores and libraries are filled with such books, and if you need practical suggestions for what to do to manage your human capital, start there. I can only say that since it is your career, you do need to take the initiative on developing it. Again, you are your biggest investment, and nothing else in your portfolio comes as close to being under your control as this one does. You *can* profit from what you *can* control, so investing in your own human capital is worth every penny.

The Bottom Line

If you measure it in terms of your lifetime earning capacity, your human capital is your most valuable asset. Think about yourself as human capital and find ways to increase its value. Your human capital is your principal means to provide for your needs and aspirations. It is also your means for creating and increasing your financial capital. We call that savings. More than any other investment you'll make, your human capital investment is within your control.

The modern, knowledge-based economy demands well-developed skills in the STEM disciplines—science, technology, engineering, mathematics—in which U.S. education lags. You'll need some competence in these subjects.

To achieve the highest value of your human capital, you'll need to augment technical knowledge with skills of critical analysis, problem solving, and creative thinking. The much-maligned liberal arts—histories, social science, literature, fine arts—are the means to develop these skills. Think of yourself as a company you might invest in: What edge or advantage would make you decide to invest in yourself? Build your brand around that, and market yourself.

Financial investing cannot rescue you from the need to develop your human capital, but it can provide returns beyond what your own labor income can achieve.

Chapter 9

MoneyShift: Getting Results

From the start, nine chapters ago, it has been our purpose to jettison past perceptions that no longer apply to the world of investing, look at the facts of how that world works today, and think afresh about how to prosper from the facts.

To that end, we've taken a cold, hard look at the political, demographic, and financial realities that have virtually inverted the direction of economic growth and power in the world, in the process painting a new picture of where and how wealth will be created. We have explored why the new reality requires a new investment strategy that itself turns the old strategy on its head. We have crossed geographic and conceptual borders to examine the new engines of growth in both emerging and developed economies, have considered anew the alternatives to equities that can support our prosperity goals, and have reminded ourselves of the role of our own human capital in gaining the prosperity we seek. It is time, therefore, to put it all together and get right down to allocating—or reallocating—assets and creating an investment portfolio that will succeed in bringing us that prosperity.

It turns out that in that endeavor also, we need to free ourselves of old thinking and start from scratch. The classic models of asset allocation are no longer relevant and therefore no longer pertinent. Here, too, we need to disenthrall ourselves, and this particular disenthrallment is likely to take some doing. That's because, whether we know it or not, the asset allocation model we've been in thrall to for so long has profoundly shaped the way we all think about investing, so we'll really have to break a shell to get a fresh perspective, and that won't be easy.

The textbook model derives from a powerful academic construct called modern portfolio theory (MPT), which won for its developer, Harry Markowitz, the Nobel Memorial Prize in Economic Sciences in 1990, decades after he first developed the model. During that time, MPT became practically the universal guide to investing. If you ever answered questions about your risk tolerance and about your expectations of future investment opportunities, then plugged the data into a program that cranked out an investment plan for you, you can be pretty sure that some version of MPT algorithms sat between your hopes and fears and a list of investment choices fitted to your profile.

So it's important to take a closer look at MPT—first, to understand how and why it became so omnipresent a practical application; second, because it offers a useful framework for figuring out our new investment strategy; and finally, because we need to get beyond this venerable academic beast and the hold it has exercised over you, me, and our investment strategies.

Modern Portfolio Theory—Laudable but with Limitations

Harry Markowitz was a graduate student in economics at the University of Chicago when he first began looking at the mathematical impact of risk on stock prices. His work in this area, which he continued to refine for years, resulted in the formulation of MPT and the 1990 Nobel Prize. But in addition to giving the good professor a trip to Stockholm, MPT has helped countless professional asset managers win mandates to invest billions and billions of dollars' worth of assets held by pension funds, endowments, governments, and individuals. John Maynard Keynes is frequently quoted as saying that "even the most practical man of affairs is usually in the thrall of the ideas of some long-dead economist." Professor Markowitz is in his mid-eighties as I write this, and I wish him continued long life, but I believe that, practically speaking, it may be time to move on from his ideas when we begin to construct portfolios of financial assets.

What makes MPT so compelling? Simply put, it solves a basic problem all investors face: how to balance risk and return. We all know that if nothing is ventured, nothing can be gained, but we'd like to figure out how to venture as little as possible in order to gain as much as possible. Getting that right is what investors call heaven and what finance professors call an efficient portfolio, and that's where the mathematical tool known as *mean-variance optimization* comes into the picture. Don't be put off by the jargon. Here's all it means:

We start with a menu of portfolios, each with different mixes of assets in them. We calculate the average (mean) return for the assets in each portfolio and figure out the risk (variance) in returns we can expect for each portfolio. When I say variance, I mean the distance from the mean; that is, how far away—how spread out—the possible results of an investment are from the average of all those results. Once we've got that, we're going to pick out the assets that give us the highest expected average (mean) return for each level of risk—the mean-variance optimization—and throw away everything else. We call our new, smaller menu of portfolios the *efficient frontier* because, having thrown away the "everything else," we have arrived at the edge of how much we can expect to make for a range of acceptable levels of risk. In other words, we've figured out how to answer either or both of the following questions: For a given amount of risk, what are the choices of assets that will yield the best portfolio return? Or: for a given expectation of return, which assets will give me the least risk?

There was—and is—something aesthetically pleasing about the balance this theory achieves—something downright elegant, in fact—and the results it produced were equally pleasing and elegant. Once we define risk as variance, we can measure it in various ways to provide us with different pieces of information. We can even quantify how much the dispersion changes when we package two or more investments together—that is, how the distance from the mean can become either longer or shorter, and by how much. In other words, we can quantify how much the zigs of one balance the zags of another. The end result is one nice, neat number that sums up all the zigs and zags into a measure of portfolio risk. It means we can know how much riskier one portfolio is than another and can compare those relative risks to the relative returns of the portfolios. And obviously, once we know all that, we can make asset allocation decisions like the rational actors that economists want us to be.

Throughout the Great Moderation, in fact, this theory of portfolio optimization served up the closest thing there was to a free lunch that finance professionals could offer. So why did Nassim Nicholas Taleb, the mathematician-epistemologist-philosopher-megainvestor who wrote the influential 2007 book, *The Black Swan: The Impact of the Highly Improbable*, suggest that investors sue the Swedish central bank for awarding MPT's authors the Nobel Prize?[1] The reason is that neat statistical formulas extrapolating historical results based on easily classifiable asset categories couldn't cope with the disruption that followed from the recent series of financial, economic, and fiscal crises.

Remember the old joke—yes, this is the promised second joke in the book—about the person who happens on someone down on his hands and knees patting the sidewalk under a streetlamp?

What are you looking for?
My watch.
I'll help. Did you lose it right around here?
No. Actually, I lost it across the street, but the light's better over here.

Like the fellow with the lost watch, many of us have looked for portfolio strategy where the data are more plentiful and the statistical methods more robust—not where the economic reality of investing really lies. For all its virtues, MPT can obscure economic realities that affect both us and the opportunities we can choose to invest in.

One way in which we limit our search to the sidewalk just below the streetlamp is the kind of classification we typically use to distinguish one asset class from another. MPT-driven asset allocation models tend to do this based on the famous style boxes we talked about in Chapter 7. For example, I can find a data service that will tell me if a company is distinguished by its fast earnings growth—a so-called growth company— or by its low market price relative to some measure of what it should be worth—a so-called value company. If I invest in a few of each or build a portfolio with many of each, have I really diversified the economic reality of my portfolio? Have I done anything to balance the risks and opportunities that come from the dynamic but volatile growth of the emerging economies or from the shifting demographics of the advanced economies? Maybe or maybe not, but it was sure easy to measure.

A second problem with mechanically using MPT-based allocations for our personal portfolios is that it really wasn't developed with us in mind. Let's not blame the tool because we tried to use it for an ill-suited purpose, but like most finance theories and their applications, MPT works from the perspective of institutional rather than individual investors. Institutional investors—insurance companies, pension funds, and the like—typically have but one actuarially identifiable liability stream. Because they're obligated to pay for well-defined expenses for a large sample of people, they can do a reasonable job of setting specific investment objectives. An insurer can pretty well estimate the investment results its treasury will need in future years to pay claims for car accidents or deaths. Similarly, a pension manager can fairly easily estimate how much is needed in the investment kitty to pay the monthly allotments due to the employees who retired after 35 years with the company. If you know those kinds of things, knowing how much on average you'll get from a portfolio of investments and how far results may deviate from that average is highly valuable information. If you're not an insurance company or a pension fund, that information is less helpful.

The liability streams that individual retail investors confront are way more complex because individual lives are more complicated than the lives of huge institutions. When I have a car accident, paying the claim is a statistically predictable expense for my insurance company, but covering the deductible is a cash drain for me that I had no way of forecasting. An individual's liabilities, rather than being defined by actuarial tables, comprise all the things that a real human being needs and wants to pay for now and in the future, a future that is going to cycle through a number of different phases on a thoroughly unpredictable, utterly unstable schedule.

Such complexity does not lend itself all that well to an interactive questionnaire asking questions that can only be answered yes or no or by checking either A, B, or C. What's my risk tolerance? We can discuss it, but I doubt that my answer easily translates into a single measure of the standard deviation of returns. What I do know, even without being told by the latest behavioral finance studies, is that the pain of losing holds a lot more weight for me than the pleasure of gaining.

Then there is the huge problem of historical data. The disciples of hard data are probably more able to control the emotional tendencies that might exaggerate whatever financial shock hit them most recently. And students of history are also perhaps less likely to be either nostalgic or fearful that some historical period—the Depression, the 1970s, the Great Moderation—might repeat itself. But which historical period should we use in answering the interactive questionnaire? Unfortunately, like the person looking for the watch, we tend to use those eras for which the data are most plentiful, a view that typically overestimates the importance of the past few decades. As the old saying goes, it's a GIGO situation: garbage in, garbage out.

And, when looking at historical patterns, are we assuming that markets—and investors—are rational? Perhaps they are, over the long term. But what somebody else defines as long term may be well beyond the moment when the bill comes due for that dream wedding you proudly agreed to finance. What do you do, for example, when virtually all asset classes, however economically unrelated, however historically uncorrelated, react in the same way at the same time and then reverse themselves? This phenomenon has become so common in recent years, usually in response to some political headline, that it now has a name. It's called a risk on/risk off market pattern—and yes, in conversation, people do pronounce it RoRo. Put it this way: Even if markets are perfectly rational, human life is not. So there is a fairly jarring disconnect between the neat, fill-in-the-box asset allocation programs on your computer screen and the reality of your investment life. Complex indeed.

Why have I distracted you with a theory that doesn't seem to get us very far? The reason to pay attention to MPT is for the questions it addresses, not for the less helpful ways in which it has been put into practice. MPT causes us to stop thinking about our investments as a bunch of good ideas and forces us to define them as a portfolio of risks and returns that can offset and complement each other. Then we have to confront the question as to whether that portfolio is a good match for the uses to which we will eventually put the wealth we expect it to generate—something we call prosperity. At the very least, therefore, classic MPT is a valuable discipline for us as investors.

So in no way am I suggesting that we cashier it wholesale. Whatever the limitations of the model as a guide to asset allocation, the risk/return relationship that is the core of the theory remains the central investment issue for the individual as well as for institutional investors.

But while the risk/return relationship continues to be a vital consideration in any investment decision, the terms for the individual investor are different from those that hold true for the institutional investor. For an insurance company, risk may mean annoying its customers with a premium hike—assuming anyone noticed that the price just got raised. For the individual retail investor, by contrast, risk means maybe not having enough money to meet the financial necessities for which you are responsible or to fulfill the aspirations you've developed over a lifetime. And asset allocation for portfolio construction means giving yourself a lifetime of purchasing power so you can pay for those liabilities without running out of money.

That's precisely what we address in this chapter: results. Putting to work the savings from your labor income to yield purchasing power returns greater than your labor alone can provide. If at some point you found yourself paralyzed by fears about China or Europe or the United States turning into Japan, or the White House turning back to the Republicans or the White House turning back to the Democrats, you can overcome those fears, which is why you're reading this book. So it's time to act now to put together—more likely, to reallocate—your own portfolio.

I am not speaking only of a portfolio of securities but rather of a portfolio of wealth—net wealth, assets minus liabilities to be precise. What does this wealth portfolio consist of? Very importantly, it includes your debts, which, unless they are tied to an investment, do nothing but take your wealth away. For many of us, the single best investment we can make is to eliminate any unproductive debt—that is, debt incurred solely to consume—that detracts from our wealth. We want to be in the business of collecting interest payments, not making them. If you have credit card debt, put the book down, pay off the credit card companies, and then come back and plan what you'll do with the assets in your wealth portfolio. (For more on how to create a plan, see the tip on Your Financial Plan later in this chapter.)

Those assets include your human capital, as discussed in Chapter 8, plus real property, insurance, any retirement pensions (including Social Security), and your financial investments of every sort. In this chapter, we discuss how to align these assets with both your fears and your hopes in order to increase your lifetime purchasing power, augment your overall wealth, and advance your prosperity.

What is the particular prosperity you seek? What risk will you run to get it? What assets and resources can you offer to achieve it? Answer all those questions, and you'll be well positioned to find the right investments for your portfolio.

Let's start by defining our terms.

Whose Prosperity Is It, Anyway?

Prosperity is subjective, even idiosyncratic. Ask 10 people what constitutes prosperity, and you'll get 10 different answers. Ask a single person the question 10 different times, and you might get 20 different answers—even more.

Yet the question may be simply put: What do you want money *for*? What do you worry you won't do or support or own because you don't have enough money for it? How much do you need to have in reserve before you can begin to enjoy the rest? Think of these answers as your life's liabilities—your spending needs and goals.

You'll find they fall into a hierarchy of priorities. You would love to own a yacht some day, but relative to putting food on the table next week or staying in the home you now occupy, the yacht is a fairly low priority. You'll treat the money you allocate toward the yacht—lottery tickets, anyone?—differently from the food and rent money.

Most of us have by now sat down and listed the major costs we need, expect, or hope to fund in the future. (If not, it's time to do so; if you have such a list, it couldn't hurt to review it.) We know the major items: college tuition, a secure retirement, periodic vacations (family and otherwise), maybe a second home, and of course a reserve fund for emergencies. So it goes, as you establish in your mind the things you want money for and your own subjective and idiosyncratic ranking of them.

The purpose in reviewing this list is not to produce a multidecade expense budget. Life is not an actuarial table—thank heaven—and living is simply too unpredictable for such a budget exercise to have much value. I remember a day in early 1985 when my wife and I realized that we were going have our third child less than three years after we had had our first (what was causing that to keep happening, anyway?), and we also realized that there would be an August in about 2002 when we'd have to come up with what was then about $90,000 (it would grow to about $120,000) in college tuition checks. That would have sent any multidecade budget out the window in a flash.

You can try to schedule your liabilities so that you can begin to fit unpredictability into a portfolio of assets meant to fund them. To fund those items on the list that are coming sooner and may be inescapable necessities, the most appropriate asset is your own human capital and the surplus you can save from your own labor income. To fund the most distant and most dispensable of investment objectives, allocate the riskiest and potentially highest-return assets in your portfolio. And of course that time line will change and your asset mix will change with it. Maybe a basketball scholarship would have given a Webman offspring a free ride through college and diverted some tuition money toward the yacht (didn't happen).

This same exercise helps you think more clearly about risk because it recognizes that you don't have one level of risk tolerance in the way you have, for example, one color of eyes. If you have targeted a portion of your portfolio to buy that yacht in 15 years and the returns fall short, that's a loss that is likely to disappoint you. If you have targeted the investment to pay for your child's college tuition and it loses, that is likely to have a more profound impact on your aspirations for your family, even on your relationship with your child. The losses may be quantitatively equal, but they are qualitatively worlds apart. You will risk loss more readily—and you will risk a bigger loss—for the yacht than for the college tuition. Like the objectives that represent the return you seek on your investments—the liabilities or spending requirements you want to have—you must segment risk into your own subjective and idiosyncratic hierarchy of priorities.

You find that hierarchy by deciding whether the loss of the objective would be more painful than the potential gain would be pleasurable. How painful would it be to not have enough money to live your desired lifestyle now? Or to not meet the college tuition bill? Or to not be able to seize an opportunity to buy a house or start a business? Or to not get through an emergency? Or to not buy that yacht?

Put the two lists together: the return you seek on your investments and the risks you'll live with to get that return. That's your subjective and idiosyncratic risk/return relationship—your personal portfolio of liabilities, understood as the spending requirements you want to have in your life. It tells you what you believe is the most you can get for the smallest chance you won't get it. It should form the basis of your asset allocation process.

This approach also helps to answer the question: "How much should I put aside now?" If you were part of my parents' generation and came of age during the Great Depression, you knew the answer: You should put aside as much as you can while still keeping a roof over your head. I sometimes worry that today's 20-somethings will be telling their grandchildren something similar, but for most of us, the trade-off between what we can enjoy now and what we might hope to enjoy or need in the future is a real one and needs to be addressed thoughtfully.

One reason it's important to set these priorities is that investing isn't free. It is the perfect definition of deferred gratification—putting off spending today for greater spending in the future. Remember the fable of the grasshopper and the ant? The former whiled away the summer chirping prettily, while the latter worked hard to store up food for the winter. It did not end well for the grasshopper. Moral: Idleness doesn't pay, and a penny saved is a penny earned. We've made saving a virtue even though, statistically at least, most of us are sinners. The virtue of setting priorities among our investment objectives is that doing so tells us how much we should deny ourselves now for the opportunity to enjoy something later. We should save more aggressively for next month's rent than for the yacht. And the risk we take with our savings also varies with the importance of the objective. Next month's rent must remain safe and liquid; the yacht account can be a pie in the sky. Again: lottery tickets, anyone?

So let's take a look at the various categories of investments we can match against these priorities of future gratification.

Portfolio You

What are the wealth resources—the assets—you can bring to bear to realize your spending requirements and achieve the prosperity you seek? Let's start with your own value as a wealth-producing asset.

My father-in-law has long told me of his disdain for the stock market. In his view, the only people who can make money in stocks are the scoundrels who buy and sell based on inside information or employ other crooked means to beat the little guy. Instead, he has built his financial plan and a comfortable retirement on a foundation consisting almost entirely of municipal bonds. Neither the fact that I can name numerous equity investors who owe their success to thoughtful and diligent analysis of information that's available to any of us nor the occasional blemish that appears on the face of municipal finance will shake his faith in munis.

And those facts shouldn't change his investment strategy even if his son-in-law actually did know something about investments. That's because in his case, high-quality bonds served as an effective hedge to what was for many years an overweighting in a successful equity investment portfolio. His particular equity investment happened not to be in companies listed on some stock exchange but rather in a small business he owned with his brother. The value of his investment grew over the years because of the work, brainpower, and careful management the siblings continued to add to this cornerstone investment. This was an equity portfolio that was as undiversified as it gets, but it did what stock ownership needs to do in a portfolio—namely, build wealth.

No, I'm not taking a family argument public in hopes of winning it. In fact, having hedged that overweight investment in himself with the investments in municipal bonds, my father-in-law may be said to have won his goal of a comfortable retirement. Rather, I want to make the point that your portfolio of wealth begins with you. Start with your own human capital, the most significant asset you have, and ask yourself what kind of an asset you are. If an asset is worth the present value of all its future earnings, adjusted for the certainty of those earnings—let's call it the discounted present value of future earnings—how do you value yourself in a portfolio? Begin by determining whether you are a stock or a bond. Once you know that, you'll have a good basis for deciding how you should diversify what is probably your most valuable asset and fund your financial needs and hopes over your lifetime.

A stock is an asset that provides a variable payout that is often larger tomorrow than today, but in return it offers substantive potential for upside. If you are a small business owner, work on commission, earn a minimal salary but with the chance for a big bonus, or are perhaps in a hot start-up venture offering stock options in lieu of a steady paycheck, you're a stock. Your financial performance may be spotty, up and down, volatile, but you're a long-term player, and in due course your career could endow you with considerable wealth.

A bond, by contrast, offers steady performance, perhaps indexed to inflation, that may offer a higher return because the future is less certain, but that promises no fireworks. If you're on the traditional corporate ladder, work in a factory or on the line in the field, or are a tenured teacher or civil servant, you're a bond. You have limited latitude to grow your wealth and limited exposure to changing conditions—which is probably good when times are bad, but not so good when the economy catches fire.

Whichever you are, you're probably reading this book because the discounted present value of your own future earnings isn't sufficient to meet that portfolio of hopes and needs we've just discussed. That is, on your own, the present value of your human capital may not be sufficient to achieve your prosperity goals. This might be because you're a highly volatile stock with an uncertain but exciting future that reduces today's value. Or it might be because you're a low-coupon bond that generates too little to satisfy the eventual cost of your aspirations. That is why you seek to complement your own labor with investments in financial assets. If you're a bond, your financial portfolio can emphasize stocks. If you're a stock, think about hedging your income risk with investments in bonds. As you add these assets to your portfolio, however, it is important to see them as tools with very specific capabilities for funding the objectives you've identified for yourself.

Your Financial Plan

If you found this book in a bookstore or from an Internet search, the keyword or shelf label was probably "investments." Fair enough; I've talked a lot about investment opportunities, about those that have vanished and about where to look for new ones, but achieving a satisfactory level of prosperity doesn't start with a search for great investment ideas. It starts with a plan, your plan. You cannot decide whether to put your money under the mattress, into a securities portfolio, or on the roulette table until you've figured out what that money is expected to buy and when it's expected to do so. So before you begin to develop an investment plan, you need a life plan. Before you start to structure your assets, try to understand the structure of your liabilities.

We all want to invest to prosper—no, to get rich—and we want our investments to get us there. We want this in a generalized, I've-been-rich-and-I've-been-poor-and-rich-is-better kind of way. Our investment objectives resemble the trade union boss who, when asked what his workers demanded, responded simply, "More." But like the unionists who eventually confronted the fact that "more" didn't always jibe with the business they were working in and in fact threatened its survival, we have to be realistic about what our investments really can and cannot do for us. To do that, we need a plan for a lifetime of spending. Of course much of what matters is unknowable, but what is knowable about the amount and timing of our eventual spending needs and wants is a critical first step toward thinking seriously about the investments that must someday fund those expenditures.

So the first step in planning is to lay out, as best you can, however imperfectly, the obligations and hopes your future holds. Then assign a weight to each of those liabilities that measures how far away and how critical it is. You may well have to edit this plan once you've articulated it. You may discover that an objective, particularly one you scheduled for the near future, is actually and unfortunately out of reach. If, for example, you can pay for that Mediterranean cruise only by taking a risky bet with a chunk of the college tuition fund, maybe it's the objective rather than the asset allocation that needs changing. The ATM machine on the bathroom wall, and the assumption that risky assets must always appreciate in value, took the phrase "I can't afford it" out of our vocabulary. It's back now. If you find you either have to deny yourself some measure of current consumption or have to forgo the opportunity to realize future gains from well-chosen risk now, you're guilty of poor liability planning—in either or both cases.

Did I say "structure your assets"? Few of us have thought about our investments in a structured way. We've followed some good ideas—*Hey, the newly rich of Asia are buying a lot of European luxury goods; maybe I should own the stock as well as the pocketbook*—and we've clung to some bad ones, but we probably haven't thought about our investments as a series of future cash flows and considered the likelihood of their actually being there as expected.

Here's a way to start structuring the way you think about your assets: Some companies allow or even require their higher-paid

(Continued)

employees to defer some of their current compensation to a series of scheduled future payments. Plans like this may have tax advantages for the employee, help the company's current cash flow, and give executives a long-term stake in the company's well-being—all good things, but they also, incidentally, give a structure to the employee's assets. Do that with your own financial holdings. Pretend they are to be liquidated according to a schedule you now specify. How much appreciation can you assume? How much volatility can you expect? How easily can you use any of them for current cash needs?

Start with your own earning potential. How much does it amount to? How dependably can you rely on it? For how long? What are you doing to enhance it?

Supplement this year's earnings with a reserve of enough saved cash to cover a full year of expenditures.

Own income-producing investments—bonds that at least beat current inflation, and dividend-paying stocks—so as to:

- Gradually compound wealth for important, medium-range objectives.
- Supplement income, especially once you've stopped earning it by the sweat of your brow.
- Help cover the rising cost of imported goods and services.

Own reasonably priced stocks with earnings growth potential so as to:

- Fund more distant objectives.
- Make you even more comfortable if you've already slotted assets against nearer-term, higher-necessity obligations.

Add some insurance in order to:

- Hold value if riskier assets go through a prolonged slump.
- Hold value if inflation steals your purchasing power.

After you've done all of these things, have some fun with investing. Travel, read, argue, and find great investment ideas that will pay handsomely if you're right and won't diminish your ability to meet your obligations if you're not.

That's what I mean by structuring your financial assets. Have I left a lot out? Of course, these are only the basic elements of an asset structure, a beginning, but they give you direction in how to understand what you own and what you may want to own. The hard part that follows is filling in the structure according to your age, your earning capacity, and your responsibilities.

Notice that I didn't ask the standard question, "What's your risk tolerance?" I think that question is nonsense when it's asked without regard to the depth of your resources and the extent of your obligations. I'm sure psychologists have ways of comparing you and me and our relative propensity to go bungee jumping, and if you like bungee jumping more than I do, you might be more likely to lay your "have some fun" assets on the roulette table than I am. But ability to take risk in the core of our portfolio is a matter of how crucial and how proximate is our next set of financial obligations. That's why assets need to be planned around liabilities, not picked out of thin air or from a mean-variance optimization model.

Getting these structures right will be hard work. And that's work you must do before you start figuring out how you'll populate those asset categories with investment ideas, which has been the primary focus of this book.

Trying Not to Lose the Money

One objective I've heard expressed a lot over the past few years from investors and their financial advisors goes something like this: "Stop telling me how to make money. Just tell me how to avoid losing any more." This understandable disinclination to watch your principal balance fall month by month explains why more and more money continues to flow to bond funds even as yields sink lower and lower. In fact, the first category of investment we should identify is one with the capability to help keep you from losing the wealth you already have. Actually, that's a misstatement:

What we really want is an investment that can't lose its purchasing power. I hate to break it to you, but there's no such thing.

What about inflation-indexed bonds? Don't they combine the creditworthiness of the U.S. government with protection against rising inflation? Treasury Inflation-Protected Securities (TIPS, as they are routinely called) do counterbalance inflation as measured by the consumer price index (CPI), that index of prices for a market basket of representative items we all pay for pretty regularly (food, clothing, shelter, energy, etc.). When the CPI rises, the principal in your TIPS also increases. The opposite is also the case, however: In times of deflation, your principal decreases. At maturity, a TIPS bond pays out either the adjusted principal or the original principal, whichever is greater. Held to maturity, therefore, TIPS do a good job of keeping your purchasing power constant. But they are not the truly risk-free investment some have claimed they are. We know this because of two factors: (1) the market value of a bond falls when market interest rates rise, and (2) inflation is only one reason market interest rates rise. Rising credit risk (just ask the Italians) and competition from other uses for money (rising *real* rates) can drive up interest rates and drive down bond prices—including TIPS prices—while inflation doesn't budge. Moreover, with today's TIPS yields reflecting both the overall depressed yields on U.S. Treasury debt and a premium price some investors are paying to calm their fears of impending inflation, the current return on TIPS is tiny. And, depending on the kind of account you hold them in, TIPS may also have tax implications that are important to evaluate.

You might use a series of TIPS to fund liabilities you know you'll have sometime in the future—those tuition payments, for example—but they won't build wealth beyond that target. And keep in mind with respect to the collegiate example that education costs have risen faster than overall CPI. That means that you might need to supplement those maturing TIPS with other sources of ready cash.

So we still need a dependable source of liquidity for known and unexpected, feared and desired near-term expenses: next month's rent, the flooded basement, or the annoying nephew's destination wedding— to travel to at your own expense, of course—at some swanky resort in the Caribbean. (It'll cost you whether you shell out for the affair or spring for a too-expensive present because you feel guilty for not going.) Unfortunately, in today's topsy-turvy markets, the definition of liquidity has narrowed. High-quality bonds and blue-chip stocks have been and continue to be liquid in the sense that you can always sell them, but at what price? You will pay a price in decaying purchasing power for holding cash whether it's under the mattress or in a near-zero-yielding bank or money market account, but I'm afraid that is the price you must pay to keep your long-term investments long-term.

So that is the part of investing that's about managing to stand pat or at least not fall dangerously behind. What about investments that can actually make things better? You didn't read this far to find out your only hope is to work harder than you are working now. You can get ahead—prosper—by investing, and there really are only two ways to do so. The fun one—buy low, sell high—we'll get to shortly, but first we need to go back to the first principle of the first finance course anyone ever slept through: compound interest.

Cheers for Compounding

Financial investments can grow your wealth through compounding. It happens steadily and without your having to lift a finger, albeit at a glacial pace. Ben Franklin gives us what may be the most trenchant definition of compounding: "Money makes money," said Franklin with his usual precision, "and the money money makes makes more money." Owning an investment that pays you a regular sum of money and using that money to buy more of that cash-paying investment creates exponential financial growth over time.[2] It's why your grandparents may well have opened a savings account for you the day you were born or gifted you with a savings bond, traditionally in the forefront of this investment role, every birthday. And it works. Consistently reinvesting his regular coupon payments has kept my father-in-law's investment strategy in good health some 25 years after he ceased being a stealth equity investor.

The problem—and we've encountered it repeatedly—is that interest rates on high-quality bonds (less so with good-quality municipal bonds) are so low that even with the power of compounding, we risk falling behind. U.S. Treasury rates as I write this are lower than the dividend yield on stocks for the first time in about 50 years—not entirely surprising since investors have run away from equities and toward bonds.

But here's the opportunity embedded in that switch. If you can compound interest payments, why can't you compound dividend payments? Decades of higher yields and spunkier equity markets may have distracted us from the opportunity to grow wealth slowly by compounding dividends. In fact, with corporations holding unusually large amounts of cash, which doesn't do them any more good than it does us, and with corporate managements seemingly reluctant to use that cash to expand operations, could we see dividends increasing or perhaps beginning to flow from companies heretofore too proud to share their earnings with their shareholders?

There's another potential advantage in compounding dividends. In periods of moderate inflation, well-positioned companies can raise prices, revenues, and dividends as costs go up across the economy. Raking in and reinvesting those dividends as they increase in value can help keep an investment plan on track even when our old enemy, inflation, is on the prowl.

In the Market

And so finally we come to the topic that we often think of as the whole ball of investment wax—using investments to get richer. By now we have a specific meaning for "getting richer"—having more purchasing power in the future than we'd have by preserving the amounts we save from our own earnings. Seeking to *grow* purchasing power, we know, carries a higher risk of failure than does seeking to preserve what you have or can gradually accumulate by saving. That's why we've matched this portion of your wealth portfolio against your more distant and/or lower-priority objectives, and it's why you would reduce this allocation as the time during which you can expect to earn and save diminishes.

What kind of financial investments can grow our purchasing power faster than inflation can take it away? Lots of markets can have fits of rapid appreciation. Think about gold over the past few years, or residential real estate during the mid-1990s. But—and I'm repeating this for emphasis— the investments that can grow your wealth over time are investments in the creation of continuing economic value and the conversion of that value into earnings.

We devoted all those earlier chapters to narrowing the search for investments that can augment your wealth by growing earnings faster and more dependably than the market now appreciates. While complex managerial, legal, and financial considerations go into finding the most promising investments—it *is* hard work—the fundamentals most likely to matter in today's evolving world economy boil down to just three considerations. Investors should look for companies:

1. That can sell goods and services to an expanding customer base whose spending power is growing.
2. That command a premium price in those markets because they combine unique technology with powerful brands.
3. That enjoy competent and honest management.

Once you've identified investments that qualify (i.e., that meet those criteria), how will you categorize the role they assume in your portfolio? I apologize that Table 9.1 doesn't have any fancy mathematics, and I know it oversimplifies, but asset allocation for human beings essentially requires that we categorize our objects by their proximity in time and importance in fulfillment. The table illustrates what I mean.

These capabilities—maintaining liquidity, beating inflation, compounding income in the form of cash flow, and finding earnings growth—constitute the framework within which an investor can identify and balance a portfolio of appropriate and attractive investments. By that I mean investments that work within the context of the individual's aspirations for return and appetite for risk to achieve his or her prosperity goals.

But of course, nothing is attractive if it costs too much relative to its return potential. The price you pay for an investment always matters. An exuberant market, just like a panicked market, can undermine the long-term value of the best growth opportunity or sap the protective strength from a source of liquidity. And since nothing is risk-free—not TIPS or slow growth or quick liquidity or long-term earnings growth—the amount of your investment should be only up to the point where a loss could be disappointing, not past it to the point where it would be disastrous.

Table 9.1   Asset Allocation

	Sooner	**Later**
Necessity	Liquidity	Beat inflation
Aspiration	Compound cash flow	Find the expanding market

What Can Go Wrong?

What can't?

"Markets can remain irrational longer than you can stay solvent," said John Maynard Keynes, who, as you've probably figured out by now, is more often quoted than read. Certainly, markets can remain irrational longer than you or I can put off writing that college tuition check.

James Carville got a lot of the credit for Bill Clinton's successful 1992 presidential campaign because he reminded the political operatives: "It's the economy, stupid." Today we have to remind ourselves as investors that "it's the politics" (I won't apply Carville's epithet, even for rhetorical purposes, to anyone kind enough to have read this far). Today's market irrationality does not exist in an insulated economic silo; many of the issues facing investors are political and therefore not susceptible to the formulas of financial analysis. I'd point to four large political themes that need to influence our investment thinking.

More than enough has been said about the unsustainable U.S. budgetary mess and the debt mess that accompanies it. We have reached a situation that political scientist Francis Fukuyama has called "dysfunctional equilibrium."[3] That's an erudite term for political gridlock in which no one with legislative or executive power will move until someone in the opposition moves, thereby leaving everyone at a standstill. But we're not really at a standstill, because temporary measure follows temporary measure, debt piles up, and the Federal Reserve, with help from foreign exporters, remains the enabler.

My goal isn't to solve the policy problem (although I feel obligated to mention that other countries' successful experiences in unraveling debt problems look a lot like the dead-on-arrival Simpson-Bowles plan: lots of spending cuts, some tax increases). Rather, I want to view the situation from an investor's point of view and raise my concerns from that vantage.

First, don't assume that because longer-term U.S. Treasury bonds have been a safe haven so far, they will continue to hold their value. Our foreign creditors can't afford to trash the Treasuries market today—they own too many of them—but they can continue to look for other uses for their dollars. For example, they might use the dollars to acquire sources of raw materials and buy domestic peace, or, as Japan has recently agreed to do, they might use them to begin accumulating asset-denominated Chinese yuan.

That process will eventually weaken the dollar and push up interest rates, and that, in turn, raises the second investor issue: inflation. I do not consider inflation a significant near-term risk for investors; that is, I see no reason to overload our portfolios now with inflation-friendly holdings. I do suggest, however, that we keep a close eye over the next several years on how quickly the Federal Reserve reacts to hints that prices are accelerating upward, especially if the economy remains weak and employment lags. Easy money was the key policy error, among others, of the 1970s. (If you don't believe me, I recommend you listen to the perpetrator of easy money, Arthur Burns, explain his actions.)[4] In any event, be prepared to add to your inflation-protection budget if you start seeing men in leisure suits again.

Before you cash in all those T-bonds you've stashed away, consider a third major political/economic risk, the interconnectedness and vulnerability of the global financial system. We don't worry about the debt of the peripheral European countries because a couple of them might default. Greece, for example, has been in default of its sovereign debt for about half of the 183 years it has been an independent country.[5] What we worry about is that as Europe struggles to build a common economic regime to fit its (ill-conceived) common currency, a combination of fiscal stringency and tight monetary policy will depress economies in the Eurozone and beyond. Hedging against that chain of events is reason for investors to hang onto modest positions in high-quality bonds while we weather the resulting storm. As I noted earlier, U.S. Treasuries have so far filled this safe-haven role nicely, but investors may need to ask which sovereign debt issue takes the stage should budgetary issues begin to erode confidence in Uncle Sam.

The fourth concern is that today's fast-growing economies will stop emerging and begin to stagnate. What makes this concern more than a cautionary footnote to a book that has been upbeat about the potential for prosperity to spread around the globe is a phenomenon known as the middle-income trap. Sometimes, poor countries enjoy an initial period of rapid growth and widening prosperity as their labor cost advantages and natural resources lead to profits in international markets, but then, once labor costs begin to rise, domestic growth fails to replace shrinking export markets, and the economy stagnates.[6] Over the next decade, some of today's rapidly growing economies will escape this trap while others fall into it.

China, in particular, has invested heavily in domestic housing, health care, and infrastructure to shift its economy from export dependence to domestic growth. Brazil, among others, is making a similar effort; they've all read the same playbook, I suppose. But if the largest of the emerging markets fail to emerge beyond middle income—India is a particular concern—global growth will fail to meet expectations, and that could chill the plans of companies from around the globe that have bet on selling products to consumers in the emerging markets. The investor's solution? Profit from the growth that is occurring and is likely to occur in today's growth economies, but be sure that a portion of your growth portfolio profits from the strong markets we've discussed in the world's less exciting, more mature economies.

We live in a world with a high probability of low-probability events: stuff happens. Just because I can name these risks doesn't mean they are the most likely among significant unlikely events. In fact, my being able to name them probably indicates the opposite. My point is that as we learn to think more and more like portfolio managers and not like soothsayers, we begin to think about ways in which we can counter-balance the problems that might arise and leverage our good fortune. I can't control these events, but I can to learn to profit from them or in spite of them.

Now What?

What's an investor to do? The global economy is in flux, and you do not know what it will look like when it stops flowing. You can't control the things that can go wrong any more than you can affect the things that could go right. You can't dismiss what markets have done, but you shouldn't surrender to them, either. Moreover, not everything that goes wrong has an investment solution any more than everything that goes right responds to an investment initiative.

But some do, and in this book, I've tried to present those things that have a higher probability of succeeding than others. I've suggested you look away from countries, including our own, that appear economically and politically stuck, and toward more dynamic markets—just to see, at least, if there's a way you can profit from them. I've hinted that the way to think about assets is in terms of economic diversification, not statistical diversification. I've advised you to look to the equities of companies with pricing power and expanding markets, to commodities and their producers, to government bonds, and other alternatives to buttress your overall investment portfolios. And I've asserted that if an investment looks too good to be true, it is. So certainly for the spending requirements that are absolute in your personal portfolio—the college tuition, the secure retirement, and for sure next month's rent or mortgage payment—reallocate away from the too-good-to-be-true into more stable investments that may promise less but yield more surely.

You must respond to the world as it is, and in my view, these times do call for more insurance—that is, for near-cash items that deliver painfully little upside but that can pay off in the event you confront an unexpected emergency or, for that matter, come upon an intriguing opportunity.

Bottom line: If you really take this chapter to heart, you'll see that investing today is a tough assignment—challenging at the least, daunting at most.

First, you need to examine the investment decisions you've already made to find any relics of an economic and financial epoch that has passed. Which investments did you make under the assumption that the long business cycles and market stability—the Goldilocks Environment—would be right around the corner, waiting for the next Fed decision or tax-law change?

Next you need to keep in mind where and how economic value is now created and look for investments whose returns are tied to the changing world. But you won't invest in any of those exciting new ideas without developing a firm understanding of how much you're paying for your high expectations and how much is too much.

Then you'll check to be sure you have some financial insurance against trouble down the road, inflation and a prolonged economic downturn being the two most obvious perils against which some insurance is a prudent investment. To get that insurance, you'll need to study some less familiar financial vehicles and evaluate their costs in relation to the risks we face.

And before you do any of these things, you'll need to delineate as fully as you can what you expect as your eventual uses for the fruits of your work, your savings, and your investments—and when you expect to pick those fruits. No investment is a good one unless it fits your particular plan for your life's commitments and expectations. Some of those decisions may have tax or estate-planning implications, and you'd better account for them as well.

That's what I'm telling you to do, and most of us would rather undergo root canal surgery (which in my experience didn't hurt nearly as much as I'd expected) than do any of this. For that reason, and because most of us have trouble considering our own finances in an objective, unemotional manner, it is not unreasonable to look for help in making some of these decisions. Help might mean anything from selecting a fund manager for only the most obscure piece of your investment puzzle to turning your holdings over to a full-service planner and opening your statements only when you're sure they look good. Determining exactly where you need the most help—specifying your eventual financial needs, selecting specific investments, understanding less familiar port-folio alternatives, estimating tax and estate implications, or all of the above—may help you to decide what level of help you need. (And check out the tip on "Looking for Help in Building an Investment Plan" in Chapter 3.)

But no matter the level of help you get, it does not absolve you, the individual investor, from hands-on involvement in managing your portfolio. That means that you must pay attention to which way the economic winds are blowing, to the assets in your portfolio, and to the stocks and bonds and other asset classes not yet in your portfolio but possibly under consideration.

It also means exercising caution. We all know that we should buy low and sell high, but it rarely works out that way. Instead, we buy when something is on the rise and has everybody talking, then sell when it is on the way down and has everybody frightened. Gird your loins and do the exact opposite. Caution is also advised for those insurance investments I recommended, for if you overinsure today, you might lose the oppor-tunity for a higher return later. Humility must be the investor's watch-word. This is true whether others have entrusted you with billions or you are just trying to manage the few dollars you've saved from a first job.

Could things turn out better than you expect? Yes, and somewhere they will. Money hasn't gone away; it has just shifted its headquarters. Aggressive investing hasn't gone underground; it has gone overseas, and it has found enterprises you may never have thought about before. It's the world that is different—and that's something you can't change. But investing, especially if you start by investing in your own human capital, is still the best way there is to augment your prosperity. So now is the time—and I've shown you the way—to look for the investments through which you can prosper handsomely from what you can't change.

The Bottom Line

The portfolio-building techniques that sought to provide predictable investment results are another casualty of the financial crisis and the end of the Great Moderation. These techniques depended on statistical relationships among arbitrary asset categories, and the relationships proved unstable in highly volatile markets.

The zigs and the zags started marching together in close order. The centrality of assessing risk versus return in your overall portfolio nevertheless remains essential to investing.

Build a wealth portfolio, not just an investment portfolio. Subtract your debt from that wealth portfolio. Better yet, pay it off if it's not tied to an investment.

Before building or restructuring the financial portion of your wealth portfolio, define your personal hierarchy of financial priorities, which should include:

- Provision for good and bad surprises.
- Priority in importance of future spending requirements.
- Priority in time of those future spending requirements.

Match your investments with those requirements according to the risk of their meeting your return expectations.

- Start with your human capital, earning capacity, and riskiness of your earnings; that is, are you a stock or a bond?
- Provide liquidity.
- Add less risky appreciation assets—for example, those that compound cash flow.
- Only then turn to assets with higher growth potential, principally equities.
- Finish with insurance against risks to your wealth and its purchasing power.

The result is a portrait of the financial returns you seek and the risks you'll accept to achieve them.

Investing is hard work. It requires discipline and, with or without professional outside assistance, demands hands-on involvement on the part of the investor.

Further Reading

The Internet is a gold mine of websites that provide up-to-the-instant economic news and financial data. It can also be a minefield. One of the dangers of modern media, from cable television to the blogosphere, is that it's easy to avoid listening to people we don't agree with—not a good strategy for finding new ideas. Following are sites that should give everyone something to argue with and think about.

Subscription Media

- The *Wall Street Journal Online*—www.wsj.com—is by subscription only, although headlines and the latest market data are available on the home page. Apps for tablets and other devices.
- The *Financial Times*—www.ft.com—offers a hierarchy of access. News and much important data are for free; free registration grants you even more; subscriptions grant you access to all information available and via a variety of devices. I like the international (okay, British) perspective of the *FT*. I like it in large measure because I can't always guess how the *FT*'s correspondents would vote in a

187

U.S. election if they had that right. It is less and less possible to say the same, unfortunately, about their U.S. counterparts.

- *The Economist*—www.economist.com. Plenty of news and data freely accessible. As with the *FT*, *The Economist* gives a more iconoclastic view of U.S. politics, but always with the libertarian bent of its founder. The expensive country reports tend to be solid.
- The *New York Times*—www.nytimes.com—remains the newspaper of record and has added many useful business and financial features.

Free

- Bloomberg—www.bloomberg.com. You don't have to subscribe to the terminal, which offers an extraordinary number of databases and functions, to troll this website for free news and data.
- *Bloomberg Businessweek*—www.businessweek.com. The magazine online is also a Bloomberg operation.

Blogs

Here's a fairly eclectic sampling of blogs that should give everyone someone to argue with while stimulating our thinking in the process:

- The *Wall Street Journal*'s Real Time Economics blog: http://blogs.wsj.com/economics/.
- Project Syndicate: www.project-syndicate.org/series_metacategory/2 Wide variety of commentary by noted economists.
- Zero Hedge: www.zerohedge.com.
- VoxEU.org: www.voxeu.org Europe-based forum for economic opinion and debate.
- Gavyn Davies: http://blogs.ft.com/gavyndavies/#axzz1i1s2evcf.
- Martin Wolf: http://blogs.ft.com/martin-wolf-exchange/#axzz1i1s2evcf.
- Greg Mankiw: http://gregmankiw.blogspot.com/.
- *NYT* Economix: http://economix.blogs.nytimes.com/.
- TED video series (Kahneman, Gladwell, etc.): www.ted.com.
- Econbrowser: www.econbrowser.com.
- Wonkblog: www.washingtonpost.com/blogs/ezra-klein.
- Calculated Risk: www.calculatedriskblog.com/.
- Dr. Ed Yardeni's blog: http://blog.yardeni.com.

- Economist's View: http://economistsview.typepad.com/.
- *Financial Times*: http://blogs.ft.com/economistsforum/. Economics blog from the *Financial Times*.

Institutions

- www.imf.org: Website of the International Monetary Fund. In addition to administering rescue and supervisory operations for countries in financial straits, the IMF provides a wealth of financial and economic data. The IMF's semiannual Global Financial Stability Report thoroughly covers what its title says.
- www.worldbank.org: Website of the World Bank. Economic reports with emphasis on economies still aspiring to emerge.
- www.oecd.org: The Organization for Economic Cooperation and Development website provides economic reports on its core membership of advanced economies but covers the largest of the emerging economies as well.

Specialty Data

- www.mcdep.com: McDep.com website provides energy investment research on market cap and debt-to-present value of energy businesses.

Notes

Chapter 1   Where Has All the Prosperity Gone?

1. www.bea.gov/national/nipaweb/TableView.asp?SelectedTable=58&ViewSeries=
   NO&Java=no&Request3Place=N&3Place=N&FromView=YES&Freq=Year&
   FirstYear=2000&LastYear=2010&3Place=N&Update=Update&JavaBox=no.

2. Bureau of Labor Statistics, "Labor Force Statistics from the Current Population
   Survey," http://data.bls.gov/pdq/SurveyOutputServlet.

3. National Bureau of Economic Research, Inc., "US Business Cycle Expansions
   and Contractions," www.nber.org/cycles/cyclesmain.html.

4. www.nber.org/cycles/cyclesmain.html.

5. www.thepeoplehistory.com/1982.html.

6. For a thorough discussion of the subprime debacle and its historical analogues,
   see Carmen M. Reinhart and Kenneth S. Rogoff, *This Time Is Different: Eight
   Centuries of Financial Folly* (Princeton, NJ: Princeton University Press, 2010).

Chapter 2   What You Can't Control

1. Carmen M. Reinhart and Kenneth S. Rogoff, "The Aftermath of Financial
   Crises," *American Economic Review* 99, no. 2 (May 2009): 466–472.

2. Demographic estimates and projections taken from the Population Division of
   the United Nations Department of Economic and Social Affairs, *2010 Revision
   of World Population Prospects*, May 3, 2011, http://esa.un.org/unpd/wpp/
   index.htm.

3. www.time.com/time/magazine/article/0,9171,843150,00.html#ixzz1Vgt5ZAj4.

4. Zheng Liu and Mark M. Spiegel, "Boomer Retirement: Headwinds for U. S. Equity Markets?" *FRBSF Economic Letter*, August 22, 2011.

5. There is no perfect collective term to use in referring to the array of highly differentiated and geographically dispersed economies whose rapid growth is changing the world's economic geography. I'll use the term *emerging* while recognizing that some have emerged while others struggle to find their footing.

6. Statistics Bureau, Director-General for Policy Planning of Japan, *Japan Statistical Yearbook 2011*, www.stat.go.jp/english/data/nenkan/1431–19.htm.

7. Federal Reserve Board, 2007 Survey of Consumer Finances, www.federal reserve.gov/Pubs/OSS/oss2/2007/scf2007home.html. Updated February 18, 2010.

8. *World Population Prospects: The 2010 Revision*, http://esa.un.org/unpd/wpp/Sorting-Tables/tab-sorting_ageing.htm.

Chapter 3   For the New Prosperity, You'll Need a New Investment Strategy

1. It even merits attention in my friend Leonard Mlodinow's informative and entertaining book, *The Drunkard's Walk: How Randomness Rules Our Lives* (New York: Pantheon Books, 2008). It turns out Roger Maris wasn't much better than a mutual fund portfolio manager, either.

2. Daniel Kahneman, *Thinking, Fast and Slow* (New York: Farrar, Straus & Giroux, 2011).

3. Standard & Poor's, "Standard & Poor's Indices versus Active Funds Scorecard (SPIVA)," www.standardandpoors.com/indices/spiva/en/us.

4. Antti Petajisto, "Active Share and Mutual Fund Performance," December 15, 2010, available at SSRN: http://ssrn.com/abstract=1685942.

5. Jeremy J. Siegel, *The Future for Investors: Why the Tried and True Triumphs Over the Bold and New* (New York: Crown Business, 2005), 19.

6. Ibid., 27.

7. Investment Company Institute 2011, *Investment Company Fact Book* (Washington, DC: ICI, 2011), 146.

8. Carmen M. Reinhart, Jacob F. Kirkegaard, and M. Belen Sbrancia, "Financial Repression Redux," *Finance & Development* 48, no. 1 (June 2011).

9. In 2008, losing 42 percent in the Nikkei didn't seem that distinguishable from losing 39.5 percent (37 percent including dividends) in the S&P 500.

Chapter 4   Where the Wealth Is

1. For a more complete discussion of terminology and groupings of the world's most promising economies from the inventor of the term BRICs, see Jim O'Neill, *The Growth Map: Economic Opportunity in the BRICs and Beyond* (New York: Portfolio/Penguin, 2011), 97ff.

2. These highly approximate time series come from Goldman Sachs Global Investment Research, "Crossing the Rubicon: Our Investment Framework for the Next Decade," February 26, 2010, p. 30.

3. The World Bank, http://databank.worldbank.org/ddp/html-jsp/QuickView Report.jsp?RowAxis=WDI_Ctry ~ &ColAxis=WDI_Time ~ &PageAxis=WDI_ Series ~ &PageAxisCaption=Series ~ &RowAxisCaption=Country ~ &ColAxis Caption=Time ~ &NEW_REPORT_SCALE=1&NEW_REPORT_PRECI SION=0&newReport=yes&ROW_COUNT=242&COLUMN_COUNT= 26&PAGE_COUNT=1&COMMA_SEP=true.

4. Comrade Deng's conversion occurred on the road to Beijing, not Damascus, and the Chinese state remained and remains active in directing the economy. For a discussion of the state's role in China's economic emergence, see Dani Rodrik, *The Globalization Paradox: Democracy and the Future of the World Economy* (New York: W. W. Norton & Company, 2011).

5. Bureau of Economic Analysis, Interactive Input-Output Tables—This use of commodities by industries before redefinitions (1997–2009), December 12, 2010.

6. Transparency International, *Annual Report* 2010, pp. 79–80, www.trans parency.org/publications/publications/annual_reports/annual_report_2010.

7. http://hdrstats.undp.org/en/countries/profiles/IND.html.

Chapter 5   How to Read Your Shirt Label: The Myth and Reality of Investing in Emerging Markets

1. http://tiltingatwindmillsblog.blogspot.com/2011/06/spains-crippling-personal-debt.html.

2. Credit Swiss 2010 economic yearbook.

3. CIA, *The World Factbook*, https://www.cia.gov/library/publications/the-world-factbook/index.html.

4. Jim O'Neill, *The Growth Map: Economic Opportunity in the BRICs and Beyond* (New York: Portfolio/Penguin, 2011), 95.

5. Antoine van Agtmael, *The Emerging Markets Century* (New York: Free Press, 2007), 236–239.

6. Toshiyuki Matsuura and Saki Sugano, "The Effect of Relaxation of Entry Restrictions for Large-Scale Retailers on SME Performance: Evidence from Japanese Retail Census," Research Institute of Economy, Trade and Industry, 2009, www.rieti.go.jp/jp/publications/dp/09e054.pdf.

7. Bloomberg, "Alibaba's Ma 'Very Interested' in Buying Yahoo," October 2, 2012, www.bloomberg.com/news/2011–09–30/alibaba-s-jack-ma-says-he-s-very-interested-in-buying-yahoo.html.

8. World Bank sovereign debt stats.

9. Arthur Burns, "The Anguish of Central Banking." The 1979 Per Jacobsson Lecture, Belgrade, Yugoslavia, September 30, 1979, www.perjacobsson.org/lectures/1979.pdf.

10. Ernst & Young, *What Lies Beneath? The Hidden Costs of Rapid-Growth Markets; The Hidden Costs of Investing* (Ernst & Young, 2011), 26, www.ey.com/Publication/vwLUAssets/CFO_Study_Master_series_What_lies_beneath/$FILE/CFO_Study_Master_series_What_lies_beneath.pdf.

11. "Chinese Banks Race to Reduce Risk as Lending Rises," *Asia Money* 21, issue 9 (October 2010), 35.

12. Christopher Barr, "The Financial Collapse of Asia Pulp & Paper: Moral Hazard and Pressures on Forests in Indonesia and China," Center for International Forestry Research (CIFOR). Paper delivered at international symposium on The Lessons from the Chinese Forest Policy Experience, June 20–23, 2001, Dujiangyan, Sichuan Province, China, www.cifor.org/publications/pdf_files/China-Papers/Chris-Barr.pdf.

Chapter 6   There Is Still Profit Among the Rich

1. Brazil, Italy, India, and Canada are the rest of the top 10. World Bank, Gross domestic product 2010, http://siteresources.worldbank.org/DATASTATISTICS/Resources/GDP.pdf.

2. Søren Nielsen, "Dynamics of the Hearing Aid Market," circa 2010, p. 8, http://files.shareholder.com/downloads/ABEA-4C7PH1/1471090910x0x392115/e0be1288-fbc0–4ece-aa15–96d5a0432ec5/CMD3_1.pdf.

3. "Baby Boomers' Aging Future Studies Reveal All: Optimism, Drugs," *Medical News Today*, July 14, 2011, www.medicalnewstoday.com/artciels.231021.php.

4. David Court, Diana Farrell, and John E. Forsyth, "Serving Aging Baby Boomers," *McKinsey Quarterly*, November 2007, www.mckinseyquarterly.com.

5. Note that OppenheimerFunds, Inc., my employer, does not sell its own shares to the public.

6. Not that there aren't exceptions. The Japanese carmakers' late-1980s success in minting new, instant prestige brands is, however, the exception, and it's no accident that the new marques sprang from established global manufacturers.

7. U.S. Department of Transportation, Bureau of Transportation Statistics, July 2011, www.transtats.bts.gov/carriers.asp?pn=1.

Chapter 7   The New Diversification: Alternatives to What?

1. *Ibbotson SBBI 2011 Valuation Yearbook: Market Results for Stocks, Bonds, Bills, and Inflation 1926–2010* (Chicago: Morningstar, Inc., 2011), 29.

2. Keep in mind that you cannot readily buy an index. Instead, you would have bought a fund that aims to track the index, and your returns would have been reduced by the fund's expenses.

3. Remember that the market value of a bond with a fixed interest payment appreciates as the interest rate on newly issued bonds falls, and the bond's market value declines as the interest rate rises.

4. Actually, the Treasury was able to auction the bonds at a premium, and you would have paid $1,008 for your bond.

5. For simplicity's sake, I've reported price changes without regard for dividend and interest payments.

6. The actual high point occurred in October 1981 at 15¾ percent.

7. Actually, you would have had to do more than hold on to your JGBs. You would have needed to trade constantly to keep your 10-year maturity from shrinking with the passage of time, or you might have found an instrument that mimicked a 10-year constant maturity.

8. Bloomberg, April 12, 2011 (20-year period is March 31, 1991, to March 31, 2011).

9. Bloomberg, April 12, 2011.

10. Some commentators include equities among hard assets that appreciate as inflation strikes. If inflation is moderate and reasonably constant, companies can pass labor and material input costs along and maintain earnings and market value. If inflation is accelerating and uncertain, as in the 1970s, earnings prospects will be so shaky that equity prices suffer.

11. Economists might call investors' motivation "uncertainty," which refers to conditions that can't be forecast, rather than "risk," which refers to conditions that fluctuate within bounds that can be estimated reasonably well.

12. "The Renovation of the South: Liberator," 35:32, p. 126, August 11, 1865. Cited in Robert J. Shiller, "Understanding Recent Trends in House Prices and Homeownership," in *Housing, Housing Finance and Monetary Policy*, Jackson Hole Conference Series, Federal Reserve Bank of Kansas City, 2008, 85–123.

13. Federal Reserve, "Balance Sheet of Households and Nonprofit Organizations," December 8, 2011, www.federalreserve.gov/releases/z1/Current/z1r-5.pdf.

14. For an account of how one huge hedge fund did collapse, see Roger Lowenstein, *When Genius Failed: The Rise and Fall of Long-Term Capital Management* (New York: Random House, 2001).

Chapter 8   Investing in Human Capital—Yours

1. In case you've escaped having to learn the finance jargon, discounted present value represents the math behind the concept that due to compound interest a dollar today is worth more than a dollar tomorrow and a lot more than a dollar 30 years from now. Interest rates are the prices the financial markets assign to how much the value of today's money exceeds that of the future.

2. Joe Light, Mary Pilon, and Jessica Silver-Greenberg, "The Young and the Riskless," *Wall Street Journal*, November 5, 2011.

3. Ibid.

4. Janet L. Yellen, President's Speech to the Center for the Study of Democracy, University of California, Irvine, November 6, 2006.

5. Fareed Zakaria, "When Will We Learn?" *Time*, November 14, 2011, 44.

6. Norm Augustine, "The Education Our Economy Needs," *Wall Street Journal*, September 21, 2011.

Chapter 9   MoneyShift: Getting Results

1. Stephanie Baker, "'Black Swan' Author Says Investors Should Sue Nobel for Crisis," Bloomberg, October 8, 2010, www.bloomberg.com/news/2010–10–08/taleb-says-crisis-makes-nobel-panel-liable-for-legitimizing-economists.html.

2. In case you forgot the formula: Future value = Present value $\times$ (1 + Interest rate)$^{\text{Number of payments}}$.

3. Francis Fukuyama, *The Origins of Political Order: From Prehuman Times to the French Revolution* (New York: Farrar, Straus & Giroux, 2011).

4. Arthur Burns, "The Anguish of Central Banking," The 1979 Per Jacobsson Lecture, Belgrade, Yugoslavia, September 30, 1979, www.perjacobsson.org/lectures/1979.pdf.

5. Carmen M. Reinhart and Kenneth S. Rogoff, *This Time Is Different: Eight Centuries of Financial Folly* (Princeton, NJ: Princeton University Press, 2010), 98–99.

6. For a more thorough discussion of where this trap has closed and where it hasn't, see Michael Spence, *The Next Convergence: The Future of Economic Growth in a Multispeed World* (New York: Farrar, Straus & Giroux, 2011), chap. 16.

About the Author

Dr. Jerry Webman is a Senior Investment Officer and Chief Economist for OppenheimerFunds. In this capacity, Dr. Webman provides strategic viewpoints on the financial and economic markets to investment management, financial advisors, and investors. Previously, he served as Director of Fixed Income, overseeing portfolio managers, analysts, and traders.

Dr. Webman has been involved in the investment and economic markets for almost 30 years. Prior to joining OppenheimerFunds in 1996, Dr. Webman was Managing Director and Chief Investment Strategist at Prudential Mutual Funds. Dr. Webman began his finance career at Merrill Lynch Capital Markets. Previously, he was an assistant professor of politics and public affairs at the Woodrow Wilson School of International Affairs at Princeton University.

Dr. Webman is a frequent guest on Bloomberg, Fox Business, and CNBC. He holds a BA in political science, with honors, from the University of Chicago, where he graduated Phi Beta Kappa, and a PhD in political science from Yale University. He is also a CFA Charterholder.

Index